Josephi

BEYOND SURVIVAL:

ONE NURSES JOURNEY

TO HEALING

By Josephine McCall, RN BSN
ISBN: 10: 1494452901
ISBN-13: 9781494452902

DEDICATION

This book is dedicated

To all who have

Ever experienced a need to heal.

Prologue

There is a place beyond survival, where battle weary warriors and victims of abuse can reach for Solace. Where life does not carry so many hidden threats, or the weight of compromised dreams.

Where faith in self and others can be accepted without reserve, and challenges can be achieved with a sense of satisfaction. Where survival itself is not a badge worn and defiantly displayed, like an unjust weight laid upon the soul.

There is a place beyond survival. And I have been there enough times to let me know there can be resolution. That forgiveness, healing, and closure are not too high a price to pay.

Josephine McCall RN BSN
C TXU 403 976
"Petals from the Masters Bouquet" 2002

PONDER SLOWLY

THOUGHTS INSIDE,

FOR IN THESE PAGES

I ABIDE.

MEET MY NATURE,

KNOW MY SOUL.

LISTEN CLOSELY

AS I UNFOLD

UNDER YOUR FINGERTIPS.

CONTENTS

ACKNOWLEDGMENTS

I would like to give some words of thanks to a number of nurses who have provided me with understanding, insight, and support along the way. I have been blessed by your presence in my life.

To Mable Carlyle, instructor, mentor, and friend who has always encouraged me to stretch my mind, recognize my soul, and learn all that I can about life. I would like to say you were an early example of determination and focus that I sought to follow. I came to appreciate many of the similar challenges we experienced in our early years, and the varied approaches we both took to deal with what were often intense and painful issues. I thank you for all of your caring and for the many years that we have shared similar interest, tears, and ideas together. Your dedication to the Sigma Theta Tau Internationals Nurses Clinic at the homeless shelter in Asheville is what helped to keep it viable for the length of its existence. I thank you for your efforts in that nursing endeavor, and the opportunity it gave me to attempt and then succeed in gaining our chapter recognition for that work. Your explanations and understanding of human behavior, as being a result, in part, of each person's life experience, helped me to look at my own life from a different perspective. I was then able to take a number of more effective steps in the direction of healing what I had viewed as a splintered soul.

To Jeanne Howe, whose patience, excellence, and guidance often provided me with the kind of support I needed as a nursing student and as a person, I would say thank you. You were, and still are, a wonderful mentor, and I can hear your voice in the background when I am counseling nursing students in the clinical area. You gave alternative perspectives to many challenges I faced, and provided a non-judgmental sounding board on which I could explore spiritual questions I might have otherwise avoided asking. I have many time modeled this approach with others, and have found that the results have always been positive. I thank you for all of those opportunities and would have you know that I always hold you close to mind and near to my heart. Your acceptance and understanding of me as a person and a friend helped to give me needed confidence. This allowed me to take the initial steps that were required to write the first pages of this cathartic book. Your response to my efforts encouraged me forward, toward the healing of my own spirit, and then to endeavor to offer that hope to others.

To Sharon Jacques, whose encouragement and faith nudged this neophyte into filling more responsible positions in her nursing career than she might have otherwise attempted. We've shared many a ride and broad discussion about nursing, ethical issues of importance, and the changing state of the world around us (in general and particular). I appreciate the time and effort I feel you invested into my life and career. The ripples you started by tossing that pebble of interest into the water continue to the present and are likely to go on into the future. Your faith in my potential as a person and a nurse has continued to encourage me forward in my personal and professional growth. You are also one of my strongest role models. I have also enjoyed watching you climb your own ladders of success over the last few years.

To Marge Johnson, who had faith in a young girl first stepping out into the world of mental health, albeit she did see the girl as being a bit hard headed. I also owe to you a statement of gratitude. You gave this unskilled, teenage young woman a chance to take steadier steps toward adulthood. Your voice still sounds in my memory as you told me, “Joey you are an intelligent girl but sometimes you do not use your intelligence but you don‘t always make wise choices". You were one of the first nurses I met that exemplified what being a nurse was all about. By who you were and how you lived, you let me know that you can make choices in your own life and own nursing career that can be based on what you, (as a person), believe or need, and those choices do not necessarily have to be based on the directives and beliefs of others. It was a loss to this world when you died but the next world gained a worthy and experienced soul. You are missed.

To Carol Stevens, who approached teaching from a somewhat abstract angle that I immediately recognized and understood. I found in you a kindred spirit. One day in passing, you put a name to what I strove to be, and gave clarity to my efforts to reach for healing in myself and others around me. I have since seen myself as a healer and reach to share the message of hope and recovery from pain to those who are in need. I express my sincerest appreciation for that recognition, and my resulting ability to refocus on the arrow of my life. You made a difference in the lives of many of your students and especially for me. For that I thank you. Your work to get the Masters in Nursing Program at WCU started will also be long remembered and appreciated. Like a child set free, it continues to grow and evolve into something different as it goes. Wherever you go in this life you carry a gift of light that cannot help but shine on those around you. I have no doubt our paths will crisscross a number of times throughout the rest of our careers. I thank you for simply being you.

Last but not least, I want to thank the nurse who came through the doors of Highland Hospital of Asheville in the early 1980's as a client in need of treatment. You never knew, that by being there, you led by example. You sought treatment for depression, secondary to an abused childhood. You thereby gave acknowledgment and permission that it was okay for a nurse to seek counseling and help when it was needed. Through your lead I also learned I could not effectively attempt to take care of others with an abused past, until I faced and dealt with my own issues. I do not remember your name, which is appropriate, but I do remember your willingness to acknowledge your own need for treatment and then that you took the steps necessary to heal. Where ever you are I thank you from the bottom of my heart for the road map you laid for me to follow. I am hoping in some way, with this book, to offer that opportunity to others. I also hope your life, as mine, has been blessed many times over, in part, due to the healing we have allowed ourselves to achieve.

Authors Note

I have been encouraged to publish a book of my writings as a means of providing support and validation to others of similar circumstance that may also have a need to heal. Those who might benefit from this work could include; nurses who have been abused as children and continue to deal with leftover and unresolved issues, nurses who interact with clients that have a history of abuse, nursing students in need of information on and examples related to the topic of abuse, and the everyday person who has experienced physical or sexual abuse and is seeking support for the hope that there can recovery from this childhood experience.

In this manuscript, I have tried to process my own past history in a manner that would be of benefit to me and might be of help to others in understanding a measure of the confusion and distortion that abuse brought into my life. I know that others may have endured similar confusing and traumatic experiences. The emotional turmoil did not resolve when the abuse stopped. It almost felt like it took on a life of its own. It took years for me to recognize how often I was replaying scenarios from the past, and experiencing the same kind of unhealthy results. I reached a point where I realized I could not continue to live my life in such a dysfunctional manner. I finally understood it would require that I make some major changes in how I related to others, and how I perceived myself. I also realized I could not provide compassionate and empathetic care to others, including my children, until I learned to accept a measure of care and healing for myself.

INTRODUCTION

The following pages are reflections of my own life experience; as a victim of abuse, as a child abusing another child, as a child who was caught early and ceased abusing any others, as an adult who was self- labeled a survivor, and much later, as a person reaching for being more then "a survivor". I have included background information on my parentage as I feel it has some effect on how my life has gone. I started writing as a teenager, in an attempt to express a lot of mixed emotions. That grew to be a part of my own self growth and emotional healing. Within the later pages of this book are numerous poems and pieces that are results of steps and detours I made during that journey.

Writing for me became a saving grace and was a means of letting out the intense and confused feelings I often felt. In spite of the negatives I experienced, I feel I have lived a reasonably productive and fulfilling life. Hopefully I have given back (and continue to give back) a measure of the gifts and graces I have received along the way. I still deal with a few demons, but have realized I cannot undo wrongs I have done in the past. In order to move forward, I must at least acknowledge their existence in my present.

I invite you to share in some of the phases of my life. You may at times be very angry, frustrated, and ashamed of me, but probably no more so than I have been of myself. Hopefully, you may gain a different perspective on the topic of abuse. You may even learn something about yourself and your perception of those who abuse and those who have been abused (too often one has also been the other). Life is about learning from our mistakes, and if possible, moving on toward a better future for ourselves and those around us.

Chapter One
Mother

There is coffee perking on the stove and the smell of wood burning in the Warm Morning heater. There is the scent and sound of bacon frying on the cook stove and the noises of mother moving around in the kitchen can be heard through the paper thin walls of our bedroom just on the other side of the kitchen. Snow is falling and forming drifts around the outside of the house. The snow is so heavy it weights the lower branches of the tree limbs almost to the ground.

Our bedroom window is covered with ice crystals, our breath is rising out from under creases in the cover and swirls drift upward like puffs of smoke. Its Thanksgiving morning and memories of yesterday's Christmas Parade kicking off the holidays are fresh in my mind. Macy's Thanksgiving Day parade will be on television in a little while, and even if we are watching it in black and white, it will not matter to us kids after all we do have our imaginations with which to work. It was a dependable routine in our lives to have mother cook our breakfast on this holiday morning and then start our Thanksgiving dinner which would be eaten late in the afternoon.

Mother the center of our world. She was always there. Often, she was saving little critters when they got caught in traps, fell out of a tree, or crawled out from under our porch during the warm summer days. They became pets, like Rose the squirrel, Am the possum, and even the rescued wolf spider which the college professor from UNCA came to pick up for study. I can't forget its long legs sticking out from under the cup mother capped over the spider, to keep it from getting away, or the chunks of meat she dropped down into the jar where we kept it, to provide it with food which she guided to its mouth with a broom straw so "the poor little thing wouldn't starve". It always amazed me how many of the different critters we caught survived, but with time we all took it for granted that mother could save anything.

Mother the artist, on rare occasions with oil paints and brushes in her hands, working on the pirates head with eyes that followed you all around the room, or the panther watching the gazelle as it came to the watering hole to drink. The drawing of the snowman built on the winter lawn with smoke swirling from a chimney in the background was one that made it to the TV station, and was shown on Mr. Bill's cartoon morning show. There were the colored pencil drawings of a girl sitting cross legged on a multifaceted woven rug. Before Christmas, mother might be making Christmas bells out of tinfoil, or dipping prickly seed pods into gold or silver paint for tree decorations, or she might be whittling angels from a bar of soap with a knife.

Mother. Sometimes with blood on her face and bruises on her arms. Once she had a BB shot into the front of her leg, when daddy pulled the trigger on a whim. The day she came home from the hospital with our baby sister, daddy started drinking. With sister in her arms, she became a live punching bag. It didn't matter that she was weak from the delivery, and had also just had surgery. There were times when there were screams and tears that my brothers and I couldn't run from, as we tried to hide ourselves in corners on the back porch of our home. Sounds we could hear for years in our dreams and that would sometimes wake us with screams of our own in the middle of a restless night's sleep.

Mother was always trying to place herself between daddy and us children in order to draw the tangible danger to herself. Then there might be hope we would all just survive for another day. There were stormy summer afternoons when all of us children sat on the Cedar chest in the bedroom for "safety" from the lightning and the thunder. Mother would tell us stories full of pirates, sunken treasures, and small forgotten islands in strange and hidden parts of the world. Focused on the story, with the thunder and lightening as a backdrop, we didn't consciously sense the insecurity, or storms of terror she must have been battling in her own soul. Life's many conflicts have taken a toll on her body and her mind. The latter of which now frequently wanders between the past and the present, only occasionally settling anywhere in between.

Chapter Two
Her Stated History

Mother
Where my life began;

Martha Elizabeth McCurry was the youngest of 7 live children born prior to the last depression, on April 13, 1931, to Adelaide Rhodes and Joseph, McCurry. There was one daughter in the family born before mother who died shortly after her birth and another one that was reportedly still born. Mother would talk of hearing a baby cry in the house where they lived when there were no babies around. She said she thought it was one of these two child's ghosts that did not rest in peace.

Mother grew up with two brothers and three sisters and a father who was sometimes inexplicably absent from the home. Rare pictures of Mother as a child reflect an almost emaciated young girl with dark hair, bright eyes, and a very prominent nose. Mother had one picture of my grandfather and some of her siblings but none were ever available of my Grandmother. Mother seems to have inherited the size and shape of her nose from her Father.

To acknowledge Mothers story is to also validate the lives

and difficulties experienced by her siblings, and many of the families who lived in the back hills of North and South Carolina during the 1930's and 40's. Much later, when the children were in their 60's My aunt Pauline Mothers sister would send Mama many letter's full of the adventures and difficulties they had shared when they were young. Aunt Polly would make reference to the Mountain Lions that roamed in the areas around their home, and the loud screams the cats would make while moving around and underneath the house late at night. She would speak of the care that had to be taken so that you did not step on copper heads or rattlesnakes around the yards and in the fields. Aunt Polly would mention siblings who were dead, or died shortly after their birth, and her sometimes sense of having felt their presence in the home long after their demise. As Aunt Polly aged, she began to meander on various topics she discussed and situations she described, which made it more difficult to sift accurate facts from what may have been added fabrications. This tendency to wander and add fabrication was evident in many members of the family.

The distance from the family's home to the next house was said to have been many miles and traveling was usually on foot, as no one in the family owned a horse or car. Apparently, on rare occasions, if there was a need for the whole family to go anywhere away from home, the younger children might ride on the back of the milk cow, which they would always take with them. It was also important when there were things to be done away from the house that everyone finish with their work early. It was emphasized that everyone needed to be home before dark, due to the wide range of dangers that could come out of the adjacent and dark woods at night.

When I was growing up, Mother would talk of occasions when she was very young when there was little food in the house. She told of one particular incident when one of her brothers caught some minnows from a creek, and these were cooked and eaten whole. Mother described another occasion when the family had only a few potatoes, which they would peel and cook. They used the potatoes for one meal and the peelings for the next. She indicated her own Mother (my Grandmother) would walk the long distance to town to try to sell handmade woven baskets, or try to find work cleaning houses or doing laundry by hand. Grandmother might be gone for long periods of time and the children had to look out for themselves until she returned.

Mother described extended periods of time when her Father was gone from the home. Then, without explanation, he would return and be home for a number of months to years. There was not a clear reason available for why he was gone or where he went and children were not allowed or encouraged to ask questions about these absences.

When Mother was ten years old, she started to take lunch to her Father, who was at that time living at home with the family. Grandfather McCurry had previously been working on a scaffold at the front of a church. Mother stepped through the opening to where the scaffolding had stood and did not realize the scaffolding had been moved since her last visit to the church. She dropped a number of feet to the ground, breaking many of the bones in her right arm. She stated she experienced a great deal of pain from this fall. The effected arm apparently became useless to her for a time. When she was twelve years old, she had a type of surgery which she described as “something that hadn’t been tried before, where a piece of bone was removed from her leg and placed in her right arm". She was left with large scars on the right arm and leg. When the surgery was finished, her arm was fused at a right angle and she was never able to fully flex or extend that arm again. The breaks must have been severe, as she would sometimes say, "At least I got to keep my arm”, and after the surgery she was able to use the right hand again.

When her two brothers, Edward and Earnest were old

enough, they went to work in the North Carolina Conservation Corps, in camps that were set up in Transylvania County. They would come home to visit on weekends and bring with them money for the family. Mama said she "would shine their shoes for a nickel" but, likely as not, they would talk her into giving it back to them before they left to return to the camps. There seemed to be an amicable relationship between herself and her brothers. She would talk about her sisters, and described each of them as leaving home in turn at a very young age. She related what sounded like typical competitions with these siblings and with wistfulness in her voice she talked of their being able to leave the home at an early age when she as the youngest child was not able to do so.

When mother was sixteen years of age, her mother took ill and died within a few days of this unexpected sickness. During that era, the physicians still made home visits, and a doctor came to their house to treat grandmother's afflictions. Mama described her mother's death as "something that might have been avoided" if "they had given her the right kind of medicine". She related this information with a level of suspicion in her voice. With grandmother deceased, mother was then apparently shifted from one sister's home to another, often being the baby sitter to her nieces and nephews, or helping with house work around the homes in order to earn her keep.

When mother was between 17 and 18, she was living in a home with her sister Laura, Laura's husband, Jimmy, and the children in the family. They lived in the West Asheville area of Buncombe County, North Carolina. Mother attended West Asheville Baptist Church on a regular basis and one night, while attending a church meeting, she indicated she met my biological father, Joseph Graham. He had a car and on Wednesday night would sometimes give parishioners a ride home after the services were over. It seems there were some Wednesday nights when mother went to the church without a chaperon and the two of them began to spend time together alone. Joseph had been in the military and had just completed his time served, when he returned to Asheville.

A very short man of just at 5 feet, he must have stood especially tall to have been able to get into the armed services. In the one picture I have of my parents together, prior to my conception and birth, mother appeared very young, thin and brittle, dressed in faded blue jeans and a light and obviously well used blouse. Father is dressed dapper and neatly in what appears to be a new suit. It is apparent that he is a few years older than she, and he appears much more sophisticated in his presentation. She appears shy, reserved and unsmiling. He has a large grin on his face and a twinkle in his eyes. In looking at my original birth record, I must have been conceived 3 or 4 months after the date that the picture was made.

Mother related that after she became pregnant, my father had insisted she take something to try to abort the pregnancy. This was during a time when women would generally do as they were told by the men with whom they were associated and a woman rarely questioned whatever she was instructed to do. Mother says she took the pill she was given. She indicated that he was not successful as "I promptly went to the bathroom after he left and threw it up". She indicated my father was also dating other women, and stated another young woman (younger then mother by a few years) also became pregnant. If this were the case, he would have had probable encouragement by this young woman's family to marry her a few months after the pregnancy was discovered. I have never known if Mother's statements were fact or fiction. That family's first child, who was a brother to me, was born the September following my birth in January of 1950. I have no idea when the couple married nor have I ever wished to ask that question. When I was a teen, I would learn of the existence of my biological father and this other family but that was later in my history.

A few months from term, and prior to my birth, Mother went into an unwed mother's home in the West Asheville community that was close to Aunt Laura's home. She remained at this location until I was delivered. We then apparently went home to stay with Mothers oldest sister Estelle and this sister's family in a house off of Charlotte Street. We stayed with this aunt and family for a number of months, to years.

Apparently due to mama's age when her mother died and the circumstance of not having a responsible parent, she had been made a ward of the court. When I was born, I too, for a time, fell under the court's jurisdiction, and was also a ward of the court.

Chapter Three
My Early Years

My earliest memory in life is of standing at the top of a set of steep steps that led to a basement and I was crying. I could not go down to where two older children were playing. I was apparently too small to go down the steps. This was my Aunt Estelle's and Uncle Tony's house, and the children were my two cousins, Helen and Jake. Uncle Tony would be one of the few males that I would be able to depend on and trust without reserve throughout my life.

When he died it was the way he had lived, making his own choices about his own life and how much medical, or other care, he would allow for himself. From start to finish he retained as much independence and dignity as was possible for a person to do. Prior to his death a few years ago, I was fortunate enough to have been able to visit him at the home of his daughter Mary and her family in Travelers Rest, South Carolina. I was glad to be able to tell him I loved him and how much it had meant to me to have him in my life. His response had been, "I know", and he gave me an extra hug before I left his presence. I miss his support and sense of humor, even though at times it was provided at a distance. In the last Christmas card he sent me, he wrote “be happy”, and when I think of him I am often reminded of his gentle and caring manner and his kind and giving ways.

I can remember being very young and being with my grandpa McCurry as he and I walked hand in hand down the shady cobblestone sidewalk that ran beside Charlotte Street, near my Aunt Estelle’s house. I also remember the glass horse he gave me one year as a present. I had said I wanted a horse, and he said it was the best that he could do. I remember the scent of aftershave, the clean smell of the just laundered clotheshe wore, and the sight of his very prominent and probably Irish nose. He looked a lot like Jimmy Durante an older movie star and singer from the late 50’s. I remember broad shoulders and sad eyes the few times I saw him and the wide brimmed hat that always sat on his head. I sometimes compare this memory of him to his picture that has survived the years. Like a leaf from a tree, he was gone from our lives while I was young, but I still have the little glass horse he gave me and the sparse but pleasant memories he left behind.

When I was a teenager, Mother described an incident to me related to my young childhood when we lived at Aunt Estelle’s house. She stated I had gotten into some rat poison that was under my aunt's kitchen sink. I was then hospitalized for a number of days. She described my being in the hospital ward and having been hooked up to numerous IV's. Mother said I looked so very pale she thought I might die. After I recovered, I was placed in foster care with a family in Buncombe County, named the Cannons. I was later told this was a family my aunt knew. I do not know if the incident with the poison had anything to do with the change in my living situation or not. I don't know exactly how old I was and can only guess from pictures and information available from that time frame. Based on general clues I guessed that I must have been between four and five years old when this move was made.

I remember, even now, a lot about the Cannons farm and the times I spent playing in the chicken coops, and climbing the many trees in their front yard. There were other farms close by with big barns, cows, horses and large hay fields. During the time I lived at the Cannons Mother states she took a cosmetology course and received her license to practice cosmetology. I do not ever remember her working in a beauty shop, but she stated she had employment in at least one shop in Asheville. She indicated she was asked at some point to leave the beauty parlor due to her lack of experience. Mother was none the less pleased to have gained the knowledge of cosmetology and from having been able to take the course. It was probable that a grant had been provided, or a government program made available to her, as an opportunity for her to take the class and then obtain employment.

While I was in foster care, Mother would on occasion come to visit me. On a warm Saturday afternoon she came to visit while in the company of a tall man with short dark brown hair. He was dressed in green work clotheswhich were commonly used during that time period. They walked with me out to a soda shop not too far from the Cannons home on Brickyard road. We had ice cream at the shop and I was pleased with the clean look and pleasant smells of the place and of course of the ice cream. There is a snapshot that was taken of me that day that has survived the years. I looked to be a small waif with a slight frown on my face and a pout on my lips. For years after Mama would tease me that I had told them they spelled ice cream when they were trying to spell the words over my head. A short time later, they married, and I left the Cannons to live with my "parents". My stepfather adopted me, and without question, I accepted him as father. For a time I forgot that there had ever been a time without my stepfather's presence in my life.

Life can be interesting and I again spent time in this neighborhood where I had lived with the Cannon's when I dated an acquaintance of mine named Jimmy later in my adult life. He lived across the street from where the Cannon's home had been situated in those earlier years. The Cannons house was gone but the memories of the activities that took place and of the time I spent there remain. One fond memory in particular was of the large tree they had in the front yard that I liked to climb to make myself feel taller.

The legal practice of the time was to seal the original birth certificate and to make a new one with the adoptive name on it. I found out later that the second birth certificate placed my birthday a day later than the original birth certificate. As an adult, I was given a copy of that original certificate by my Aunt Estelle, and it is interesting to see the discrepancies in the two when they are placed side by side. I never really knew why she had a copy of the original birth certificate, and Mother apparently did not. The two dates also offer me the opportunity to celebrate my birthday on either or both days, should I choose to do so. My tombstone is already set up and it is the one place where I had my true birthday actually written and set in stone.

In our first few months together as a family my Mother, Step-Father and I lived in a small apartment off of Buchanan Avenue, a short street located in the Biltmore section of North

Asheville. We were in the ground floor apartment of a 3 story brick house. That is the location where we lived when I was first enrolled in elementary school. After we moved into the apartment, I had for a time, a small star nose mole I had found in the yard that I kept as a pet. I put him in a small box beside the stove and fed him raw hamburger. I think he reminded me of the freedom I had experienced while at the Cannons home. He died within a few weeks and mother left the impression that "the mole might have eaten the ashes off of daddy's cigarettes and this had caused it to die. She said he knew not to put ashes in the box with the mole". It was my first remembered experience of the loss of a pet and the first identifiable time that seeds of suspicion and distrust were planted in my thoughts by my Mother related to my Father's darker nature.

After I turned six, I started school at Vance Elementary School on Biltmore Avenue. I carried my lunch of peanut butter and jelly sandwiches to school each day. I began throwing my lunch away as I walked to school. I realized I might get free meals from the school like some of the other children in my class if I did not have any food from home with me. The teacher became concerned when I did not bring in a lunch and made sure I had the regular meals. I didn't realize she would contact Mother about her concerns, but of course she did. The paddling on the way home from school after the parent teacher conference that day reminded me not to throw my lunch away again, and not to lie to the teacher.

Being the curious type, I had also wondered what the new meat grinder might do to the knife blade I put through it. I found out when it was chewed to bits, my mom found out what I had done, and my backsides helped pay the price for my curiosity. “Ouch”.

Mother worked for a time as a house keeper and baby sitter for a family by the name of Mocks that lived in a Biltmore Forest home which was a more affluent neighborhood in the Asheville area. Mother could ride back and forth on a bus that ran past our road to the beginning of the boulevard where the family lived. This family had two children younger than me, and apparently their mother was not in good medical health. Mother would sometimes take me with her to the home and I was able to play with the two children, and spend time in the large house and yard.

The family had a television, and I can remember on occasion, watching "Our Miss Brooks" while at their house. We did not have a television at home and this was a whole new concept to me. One afternoon, I had stretched out on a couch in the den for a nap and woke up to find the youngest son (who was still in diapers) sucking on my big toe. That was a surprise to me and was something I was teased about by my parents for a long time.

The oldest son came into the house one afternoon holding a Black Widow spider by the legs. Its belly was turned up with the red hour glass shinning prominently from its middle. Mother was distraught, but managed to get the spider from his hand and dispose of it before it had an opportunity to bite him. He had no understanding of the danger he could have been in, but everyone else in the house certainly did. The adults in particular all seemed relieved when the spider was gone.

Mother took care of the children of the next door neighbors of the Mocks one particular night and I got to come with her. The neighbor had three children all of whom were boys. We had hot dogs for supper and one of the boys teased me about being the mustard man when I asked for this condiment to be handed to me to use on my hot dog. I exhibited the beginning of a temper when I started around the table to bop this boy on his nose. Mother stopped me before I could reach him. Oh the trials of childhood (not to be able to reach him and bop him on the nose like he deserved was such a disappointment).

On another day when I was there I met an older boy in the

neighborhood who had a boxcar he had made by himself from wood and string. He offered to let me ride it. I can remember waking up from a crash that occurred feeling very nauseous and dizzy. I found mother holding me and looking down at me with concern on her face. I'm not sure how long mother worked in this position in Biltmore Forest but it was a pleasant experience for me to be able to go with her to that job. I think we both were happy in that setting. I don't remember her ever working independently outside of the home again.

At that time we didn't have a television and there was not a lot to do on weekends off. On Friday nights, we were able to go to car races at the McCormick field racetrack at no charge. Anyone who was in hearing distance of the races was allowed to come in to watch the races at no cost. I can still smell the gasoline and hear the squeal of tires as they raced around the curves of the track. Mother and I usually got a hot dog, soda, and maybe popcorn. Daddy had his beer. It was lighthearted and fun for me, and as far as I knew, we all had a good time. I had yet to recognize a darker side to daddy that came out when he drank too much. Those mixed experiences were all left behind when, a few months later Mother became pregnant with my first brother and we moved to a small house on Johnston Blvd. Our house was in the same neighborhood and close to my step-Grandmothers home. We could see her house from our backyard across the span of a small valley. Our lives changed in a number of ways some of which were dramatic within that next year.

Chapter Four
Daddy

I remember a night riding on the shoulders of my stepfather when I was five years old. He carried me down an unlit boulevard in the middle of the night. We crossed a railroad track that ran for miles in both directions. I was, at the time, a child with faith. I remember being told later in life that I had asked him the first time I saw him, if he was going to be my daddy. I remember trips to the mountains and picnics with family and friends. Sometimes we attended occasional non-traditional church meetings held in out of the way places. The services at times were loud and full of fire and brimstone but I don't remember ever being frightened by them.

I remember not having to go to school for a day, as we were spending the night at his friend's house. It was too late for us to be taken home so I had an unexpected and added holiday. I remember big gardens and huge flower beds, of which he was very proud. I remember walks to the stores (we had no car), that were easy, and occasional hiking trips to the Starnes Cove fishing pond a few miles away from our home. Daddy rarely left the lake without a whole chain of fish. The strange concoction, made of unknown and foul smelling ingredients for the fish bait, was acrid, but the crust off the cornbread with butter was heaven. Daddy used the soft inside of the bread to make one of the balls of baits that he used. I remember the horn toad lizard he found and the mate we bought at the pet store so we would have a pair.

The ‘possum we named Am, who daddy rescued when its mother was killed, which we kept in a bird cage in the front room. It would open its own door to the cage in order to get out so it could make use of a box for its necessities.

This happened one time when we had an encyclopedia salesman visiting in our home. The incident scared him so badly that he left his sales samples on the couch as he took off out the front door. He did eventually come back and reclaim them, but he stayed only long enough to pick up what he left behind and then he was again gone in a hurry.

There were light cheeps during the night, a rosy glow from the light bulb in the nursery box that kept the little dibbers warm and there were soft pecks on our noses when we nuzzled the chicks close to our faces. Those were good times and fun memories. I remember occasional smiles when things were good and he was happy. I felt comforted and loved.

I remember daddy bicycling to Asheville which was a

number of miles away to his job and then his returning home late in the evening. Once he brought home a small stool that he had helped make on his job that mother and I could use to reach things from high up on the shelves. I smilingly claimed its ownership. Sometimes we would scavenge his lunch box for left over jelly biscuits and maybe find a small, round pecan pie as well. Daddy seemed caring and would often laugh at our antics around his lunchbox.

I remember the evening he came home early and decided to mow our lawn. Daddy returned to the house a short time later with blood pouring from a severed boot that had toes dangling from the edge of his foot. Some were barely attached to the foot by some skin. The lawn mower blade hadn't stopped when his foot got in the way. A neighbor took him to the hospital, but the doctor could not save all the toes, even though he tried. Daddy was fortunate to be able to keep enough of his toes to maintain his balance when he walked.

He put a tepee in the front yard and we watched TV on the lawn. We then had a drive-in movie of our own. He brought chinquapins he had picked from the woods when he would go out hunting and 6 or 8 squirrels for the pot, to make gravy for breakfast or dinner. Once he set a trap to catch Starlings in the yard, which he then cleaned and cooked. I thought it was just something new and different to try and had no idea we might have been close to starvation.

He put a roof over my head, food on the table, and brought wood for the fire. He gave a last name to a child in the need of one. In those early years, he was everything I thought a father could be to me. It changed for all of us, over time, with the poisoning of his mind by his family, the increasing amounts of alcohol he drank, and with the sexual abuse I experienced at the hands of his step-father. After a time he began to beat mother, then me, and as my brothers got a little older, he began to beat them as well. He never hit baby sister, but she still had unseen scars from verbal abuse, and she suffered much worse in her role as a child after daddy left the family and a short time later when he married the lady next door. That was so many years ago.

He is now coming to the end of his time, and I find tears on my face. I try to understand why they are there and where they are coming from. I guess we all do the best we can, and considering what he probably had to deal with in his own childhood, it was no wonder that he had his own share of demons and abusive behaviors. So I make my own peace as he passes from this world to the next, and I wish him no pain or ill. We have each lived our share of turmoil. For his willingness to care for me in the beginning, I thank him, and the rest is like leaves in the wind.

Chapter Five
Daddy's Known and Reported History

Henry Albert Sherlin was born on December 31, 1932 to Lavada and Henry Sherlin Senior, in Madison County, NC. The families were farmers of sorts, with little formal education gained by anyone in his parent's families. Theirs was a rough life, trying to manage, with little to manage on. Henry was the middle child in the family, with an older sister named Wilma and a younger brother named Bobby. When Henry was old enough, he went into the Navy and his brother followed him in a short time later. Requirements to get into the service were apparently less stringent at that time or he might have been denied admission to the Navy.

The brothers were reported to have different fathers, and his mother had married at least twice. She was said to have divorced Henry's father while the father was incarcerated in a Marshal jail. She then moved to Asheville. With the history of Moonshiners in that area of Madison County and the family history of alcoholism, it is likely that Henry Senior was arrested due to an alcohol related incident. One of the few times he came to Asheville, was one particular weekend, when he had come to visit us in our home on Johnston Blvd. I can still picture him late that night, passed out on a too small mattress on our back porch. I don't remember ever seeing him again.

At some point after the families move to Asheville, Henry's mother began working at the diner of the local bus station, where she was a waitress and sometimes cook. This is where she met and later married her last husband. He was a younger man then she by a number of years. He had apparently paid her a lot of attention when he had the opportunity. He was frequently around the bus station where he often made truck deliveries of various supply's at the bus terminals. He was a much smaller built man then her previous husband, he was very thin bodied and when we met him he was toothless. I never really knew why or how he got his nickname but everyone called him Bug.

I can remember my Step-Grandmother being in our home on occasions and having spells of "passing out". She would drop to the floor, readjust her glasses, then apparently become unresponsive and was very still. Over time I came to see her as an enemy to the family, and often a trouble maker for all of us, but in particular for mother. Sometimes her acidic words would stir daddy into an angry and frenzied state. When this occurred, one or all of us was bound to pay the consequences for her statements and actions, and his resulting frustrations.

Daddy was honorably discharged from the Navy before he had completed his full years of service. It was never really been clear why he left the service early. He had dated and apparently once been engaged to another woman before he met mother. Mother use to say she received the rings that were supposed to have been given to that woman. It was only recently that I heard this previous girlfriend had been killed in a car accident in Tennessee prior to Henrys meeting my mother. He was reported to have been present when the accident occurred, but the circumstances were vague, and no other information was ever available. He would from time to time talk about missing this woman, even after he and mother met and married, in a fond and wishful manner. I found it ironic that he was still so attached to this woman after so many years.

After we had moved to Johnston's Blvd, there were a number of times when just living could be an ordeal. One night in particular, my parents were up late, and Daddy became angry and was arguing with Mother. I had gotten up to go to the bathroom in another part of the house and had to pass through the front room where the argument was taking place. As I came back through the doorway to the room Daddy grabbed me by my hair, threw me to the floor and with pressure placed his foot upon my stomach. Within minutes, he then turned back on mother and I jumped up and ran out the door. He was behind me very quickly, with a rifle in his hands. I heard him yell at me to stop and then he shot the gun, but I never really knew if he was actually trying to shoot me, or just scare me. I was scared and all I knew was that he missed and so I kept going.

I went to a neighbor's house up the street and begged them to call the police. I was frightened and tearful. When the couple was hesitant, I remember adding to the tears in an attempt to convince them it was necessary. They were resistant to responding, as they did not want to get involved in a neighbor's problems. After the man and wife had an intense discussion, with the woman pushing for the call to be made, they did agree to notify the Sheriff's Department. The deputies arrived a short time later and I went home in their company. Daddy was not happy that the law was there, but he appeared to calm down considerably. He stated things would be ok. He was warned if a disturbance occurred again that night the law would return and they could take him to jail. After they left, he continued to glare and growl at mother and me, but that night he didn't hit either one of us again. We were finally able to go back to bed and eventually to sleep.

Daddy kept Beagle hunting dogs in a lot beside the house. If they got loose, it was automatically understood that it was my responsibility to go after them. When I did find them and bring them back, if it wasn't considered soon enough, I might receive a whipping as a reminder to find them more quickly the next time they got loose. It did not matter how far or where they went, I had to follow. I can remember being frightened I might not be able to find them, and frustrated at not being able to keep up when they had found something to chase. Sometimes cold, scratched, tired and hungry, I would come back well after dark with the dogs in tow. I was always hopeful that things would be settled and I could come in almost unnoticed. Early on, I had returned one or two times without them and received a strong punishment. I learned to return without them was not an acceptable option.

Sometimes daddy would create situations where there would be a cause to argue with mother or fuss at us kids. On one occasion, he sent my brother out to look for a knife in a holster that he said was in the yard under the swing set. My brother looked all over the area, but was not able to find it. Mother and I watched Daddy go out to the swing set and lay the knife down under a swing. He then yelled at my brother that he was just too blind and stupid to find it. It was a risk, but Mother and I called him on what we had seen. Rather I should say she called him on it and I stood at her back to give support on what we saw occur. He then stopped that particular incident of badgering my brother. We knew not to expect an explanation for his behaviors and that we were fortunate for at least that occasion, that he had stopped this angry outburst. There were few opportunities to intervene during his angry outbursts.

One morning Mother was fixing breakfast, it must have been a Saturday or Sunday, as it was full daylight and Daddy was still home. He had begun to harass her in the kitchen over some irritation he was experiencing. She was standing at the stove, stirring a pan of hot gravy which she was holding by the handle with a pot holder. As he continued to yell at her and get louder and more threatening, she turned around and pulled his belt and trousers forward and out at his waist. While looking him straight in the face, she poured the gravy down the front of his pants. His stunned look said a million words as he left the kitchen with his pants grasp out away from his waist. He did not fuss with her the rest of the day and he never harassed her again when she was in the kitchen cooking.

Daddy was in the Veterans Hospital for a couple of months when I was around thirteen. He had a pinched nerve, or slipped disc, and the physicians there had placed him in traction. I was old enough that I could go visit him from time to time, and that helped me to feel a little more grown up. Those were wonderful days for us at home, while he was at the hospital. There were no fights, we felt more relaxed, and we could watch what we wanted to on TV. I almost cried when I heard he was coming home from the hospital, as we all knew things would be going back to the previous routine. I dreaded this change, but the vacation from his presence was over.

Daddy was a hard worker and had a variety of jobs over the years. His jobs included logging, picking produce on a farm, darning socks at a mill, and working in the service department of the Advance Store putting on seat covers, changing tires and being a general handy man. This last job seemed to be one of the best ones he had during my childhood. There seemed to be enough money to get by, without so many arguments about how the money was spent. He also seemed more satisfied with the work he was doing. We kids also enjoyed being able to look around through the store and daydream while browsing through the Christmas catalogs. We saw all the advertised toys and gadgets, and knew we might have a pretty good Christmas those years.

Chapter Six
Daddy's Stepfather and the Sexual Abuse

I was eight years old, and shortly after my new baby brother was born, we were left in the care of Daddy's Step-Father "Bug", while our parents took care of business in town. This became a pattern for a couple of years, where we were left with him when there was a need for us to be baby-sat. I was still considered too young to care for my brother. He was considered too young and too small for me to watch him by myself.

Bug sexually abused me, probably from that first time we were left under his care. I have never been able to actually remember the first time it occurred which is reported by therapist to be normal for children who have been abused. The closest I have ever come to that memory, is to see the pink walls of the bathroom and to remember the feel of cold porcelain against my backsides. A later full memory of abuse is of my being on my back on a bed, looking up at the ceiling in one of the bedrooms of his home. I was unclothed from waist to legs. I looked toward the bottom of the bed to see a male adult head between my feet, and his hands were removing my socks and underpants. I looked back to the ceiling and tried to imagine myself being anywhere except in that room, and on that bed. This abuse progressed to full penetration and rape.

Over a period of time and as the abuse progressed “Bug” would sometimes say things like “how would you like to start, what would you like to do first”, emphasizing my compliance and participation in the event, and implying I had some kind of choice or control in the situation. This added to my sense of guilt, that the abuse was my fault. After each occurrence, he warned me not to tell anyone, as “he could get my mother in a lot of trouble”, and besides, “no one would believe me and if they happened to, they would realize it was my fault the situation occurred”. Knowing the loud arguments that were always happening at home and the times daddy had already beaten mother, I was afraid of the threats that Bug made. I feared for the outcome if I told anyone. I also knew that Bug was a deacon at his church (a man of the cloth) and I believed his word was likely to be seen as the truth over anything I might have said. He was also an adult, and adults were rarely questioned, simply on the words spoken by a child. Daddy had already made statements that left me with the impression I was of little value.

Years later, I would learn that an adult predator may use

every means at their disposal to seduce the children they abuse. At the time of the abuse, I only knew that even with attempts to mentally not be there, that a part of me could not leave. He began with oral sex and at eight years old, I learned you can have a physical response to abuse, whether you want to or not. That as a child I was not old or mature enough to understand that adult concept. Nor can any child understand that, later, guilty thoughts of wanting the physical sensation to happen again can come unbidden, and cause guilt for what might have otherwise been a normal response to growth in a non-abusive situation.

With this childhood experience of abuse, I learned to associate sex with shame, secrecy, fear, loss of control, and unasked for attentions. For most of my early life, I often felt shame associated with any personal memories of this abuse. Even now, I would like to turn away from what I saw, heard and felt as a child. I know now, in order to get to the other side of my childhood experiences, I must walk through these memories again. Hopefully, this time with an attitude of letting go, of forgiving myself and others who were involved.

There were occasions when Daddy would send me over to his Mother's house on some errand. Often she was away working at the bus station and her husband was at home alone. On one particular day, Daddy had struck a 'possum in the head with a piece of wood. It was stunned and bleeding, but certainly nowhere near dead. I was told to take it over to his mother's house immediately, as Bug would be glad to have it to skin and cook. I carried it upside down, holding it by the tail all the way over to my Step Grandmother's house.

The walk from one house to the other was over rough and brambly terrain, and it seemed like I would never get to the other house. During the walk, the' possum would turn its head up toward me, with blood running down its face it would bare its teeth and snarl at me. I would shake it by the tail, hard, in hopes it would turn its head back down toward the ground. I was terrified it would bite me before I could get it to my step grandmother's house. With much shaking and effort it did eventually turn its head back down toward the ground.

In addition to being afraid of being bitten, I knew the abuser was home and what to expect to happen when I got there. At times I wondered if somehow my step-father knew what was going on, and was in some way involved in creating the situation for it to occur.

Shortly after the abuse began and when there was no one else around, there were a few times when I would hear someone speak my name. It was spooky to me, and the first time it happened, I ran to mother and asked her if she had called my name. She looked surprised and said no, but she had been thinking about me. I continued to occasionally hear a voice saying my name throughout the next few years. I also found I would try to make numbers and words come out even, by adding letters or numerals to the existing number or word in my head. Later as a nurse, I learned that it is not terribly unusual for an abused child to hear voices in their head, as I had. A focus on letters and numbers can be an obsessive trait and coping mechanism that an abuse victim may use to deal with trauma and anxiety. I do know I felt less anxious when I was using these methods of distraction.

Between eleven and twelve years old and when my parents weren't home, I had begun to try to attempt to replicate the sexual sensations I had been experiencing in the abusive situation. I would sometimes read illicit material that was kept in a bureau in my parent's bedroom. This would act as a stimulus. The practice to achieve the goal of sexual release came to include my starting to abuse my brother. What might have otherwise been considered by some as childhood experimentation instead went terribly wrong, due to my following the chain of sexual abuse that I had experienced. I acted to my brother like our activity was some type of a game. Within a few weeks of starting this practice he developed what was probably a yeast infection and Mother took him to a pediatrician for treatment. She quickly recognized a possible cause for the condition and confronted me. She threatened to pour wood alcohol down my straddle if I did not tell her what was going on. Fearful, and in tears I confessed to everything that had occurred over the previous years. After this confrontation by my Mother, thankfully, I never abused anyone else again.

Two things happened immediately after this confrontation and as a result of my confession. First, I was taken by bus to the Emergency Room of the local hospital, I presume to see if I might be pregnant. I will never forget walking down the long, green, somewhat dark corridors of the hospital and smelling the strong medicinal odors that hung in the air. I was frightened of the green scrubs the staff wore, the metal gurneys scattered up and down the halls of the basement floor, and the loud noises that came from different places up and down the corridor. We went past a cafeteria where individuals of color were eating a meal on one side of the hall and those who were not of color were eating on the other side. This was the first time I had actually observed blunt and prominent segregation. Like many other parts of that day, the memory seems surreal, and distant.

When we reached the Emergency Room, Mother talked quietly to the Emergency Room physician. I felt shame, as I knew I was the topic being discussed. Then I was embarrassed and somewhat frightened as I was placed on a bed for an examination. I was then draped and left alone in the room with the physician and his associate. I then received my first adult pelvic exam. I wanted to crawl away and disappear into the floor, but that was not possible. I felt the full humiliation of having been and being labeled as sexually active. The only positive thing that came out of the situation, which I was not able to even consider or comprehend at the time, was that I was not pregnant.

This hospital visit was prior to a time when it was likely that someone like Bug would have been charged in the situation. A child's accusations within a family such as this were sometimes quietly swept to the corner. Appalachian culture was still heavy with secrecy and there were a lot of times when the established authority might look the other way, rather than address what was considered a family issue.

After the exam was accomplished, the second thing that occurred was that I was taken to stay with one of my aunt's homes to stay with she and her family. I was told I would be staying there for a few days. I perceived this as punishment and felt that no one there really wanted to have anything to do with someone like me, who had been soiled through this association with abuse. This perception was to some degree supported by my aunt's reaction and distancing from me.

I did not realize that Mother might have feared for my well being at home, due to my Step-Fathers reaction to my statements about the abuse. That he might be defensive of the person who I had identified as the abuser, as he was my Step Grandmother's husband. That perhaps my Mother might have needed time with me out of the picture, to try to deal with the repercussions from the family's open knowledge of the accusations made about Bug.

On the second day I was at my aunt's house, one of my older male cousins was sick and home from school. In walking into the bedroom where he was resting and having a general conversation with him, an accusation was made by his mother, that I had been inappropriate. From my perspective it was innocent. There was nothing in the conversation related in any manner to sex. It was not seen from that view by the adults of the home. Just walking into the bedroom was seen as inappropriate.

I was now known as "a bad girl" and anything I did might be considered suspicious. I dreaded going back home and what punishments might be waiting for me there, but I also wanted to get away from my aunt's house. I presumed she did not believe anything I said to her, nor did she evidence any visible concern over what effect the abuse might have had on me. It seemed like she really just did not want me to be there. I felt the abuser had been right and everyone did think it was my fault.

When I returned home, I could feel constant tension in the house. It was just before Easter and it was tangible that the other children had Easter Baskets but as I was no longer considered a child there was not one that had been made for me. For the rest of my life at home, I would frequently feel like I was walking on eggshells around Daddy and Mother too. Sometimes Daddy would make general statements about how bad girls could get good men into trouble. The fault was presented by him, to be mine. Again the abuser had seemed to have been right. In Daddy's eyes, I was the person with guilt and Bug had been the victim in the situation.

Bug continued to be on the fringes of our lives, as he would still bring our groceries to the house and give my parents rides to town when it was needed. I'm sure this continued association by my family with the abuser was difficult for Mother, from a number of perspectives. I have no idea what my Step Father actually thought or felt other than the defense he often displayed in Bugs favor.

On one occasion, Bug came to our home when our parents were gone. He attempted to restart the abuse. I went to the kitchen and got a large butcher knife from one of the kitchen drawers and told him no, and if he ever tried again, I would use the knife. I was terrified and I don't know if I could have carried through with the threat or not. It seemed to be enough and he never attempted to bother me again. Life went on with all the ups and downs that occur in a physically abusive and dysfunctional family setting, but, thankfully it was without the previous sexual abuse.

Chapter Seven
Elementary to High School Years

For me, there have always been mixed memories and feelings about childhood and general activity that occurred around me and within the community where we lived. It took reaching an early semblance of healing before I could begin to remember more positive and pleasant memories about that portion of my life.

From elementary school, I remember class outings, where we went to the Biltmore House, Gardens and Dairy. We had off school grounds picnics and attended the Asheville Symphony at the Civic Center. It was exciting, getting ready for and going on these trips. All of us kids were happy for an excuse to not have to go to class, and for being able to participate in the activity and outing itself. I came to feel safer and be happier when I was at school than most of the time I spent at home especially when daddy was there.

One of my regular chores at home as a child was to carry in the loads of needed wood and buckets of coal during the winter to last for the day and throughout the night. I learned to love the clean, tart smell of wood being cut and stacked, then later being burned, especially in the early fall. Our warm morning heater used both fuels. The smell of smoke was sometimes strong and acrid in the house but it generally meant we wouldn't freeze and we would feel warmth and comfort from the heater.

For a while, when I was young, our home on Johnston Blvd did not have an inside bathroom and so we used an outside toilet commonly called an outhouse. Sometimes when using that bathroom I would watch as the spiders spun webs toward the top of the house or bees would swarm to make a small nest in the rafters. It was a scary place to have to go at night and it was very cold in the winter.

In the summers, before we had a bathroom added to the back porch of the house, Mother would sometimes heat water in an oval washtub over a wood fire in the back yard. We would put on shorts or swimsuits and bathe and play in the water outside. Otherwise, we used a water basin and wash in one of the rooms of the house. There were a few times mother used this outside heating method of wood under a tub to cook beans in jars for us to have to eat in the winter.

We had four cherry trees that were close to the house and it was a game in the spring to try to pick the ripe cherries before the birds had a chance to eat them all. I can remember spitting out cherry pits at my brothers and sisters then running the other direction. Daddy raised peanuts in his garden and sometimes after they matured we would roast a pan of them in the oven and have them to snack on throughout the day. During free time in the summer and while daddy was at work, we as kids would sometimes stretch out on blankets in the back yard. We had big maple trees we used for shade and could look up through the leaves as the wind blew them back and forth. Things were sometimes peaceful during those quiet summer days and I almost felt normal at least for those short spans of time.

We had an older type of wringer washer and when the clothes were washed and rinsed, we would take them outside and use clothes pins to hang them on a clothesline to dry. The smell of the clean, dry, clothes was sweet and woodsy. One day, when I was still of a small stature and age, I was helping Mother wash the cloths. I got the fingers of my left hand caught in the wringer, while trying to put clothes through it. It continued to pull my hand and arm in, up to my shoulder, before Mother could get it stopped. I blacked out and when I woke mother had carried me to the couch. She bathed my face with a cold wash cloth, than went next door to call the Dr., but she did not take me to see him. There was probably little that could be done about the skin being rolled up on the back of the arm, or the resulting nerve damage and loss of feeling that occurred in that area secondary to the incident. Numbness to the back of that arm has continued throughout the rest of my life. It is a strange sensation when that area itches and no amount of scratching is successful in reaching through the deadened nerve endings to make it stop.

Between 8 and 11 years old, I carried an unrealistic fear of the time when I would start my menstrual cycle. I was afraid that I would be pregnant from the already experienced exposures to sex. Even if it had been a while since I had been abused, I thought I would automatically be pregnant from those past incidents. I had many misconceptions about life, sex, physical and emotional feelings, and pregnancy. It would take years to unlearn these perceptions from the misinformation I carried in my head. It would take a lifetime to deal with the effects abuse had on my thoughts and beliefs about myself and the world around me.

One of the positive outcomes of elementary school that occurred for me was that I developed a love for reading. It gave me a way of putting distance between myself and the world around me. Just before starting high school I had gotten a book that had daily positive readings in it. They were simple and could be compared to affirmations or daily devotionals about life. This was of support to me and helped me to develop at least some more positive thoughts about living. When I read the verses and notes it felt like something personal and solid I could hang on to for the day.

While still in the lower grades, I would read historical novels about the pioneers, animal stories like Black Beauty, and the Call of the Wild, and histories of wild and foreign places that helped to create colorful pictures in my mind and fuel my imagination. I looked forward to our class trips to the library and the escape from reality that I could achieve through reading. I eventually developed a love for more vivid science fiction stories as well, that has continued into adulthood and has stayed with me throughout the majority of my life. At times when I was in school I was often excited about learning something, almost anything, new.

At one point I also began to keep a simple diary and for a time would write in it almost every day. It became an outlet for many frustrations. I was a little afraid my parents might find it, but somehow felt like it was worth the risk. With this process I began what would now be called the early stages of reflective thinking. It was also the beginning of my early attempts at writing poetry.

When I was in the eighth grade, the Beatles were the rage

and the radio was full of their music. The eighth grade teacher found four of us mimicking “I want to hold your hand” off of the record player, using brooms and table tops for guitars and drums. From this incident, an idea was born for a skit to be used in the upcoming talent show that was to be held at the local high school. In the development of the presentation that followed, I was casually and without mention, replaced by a more prominent member of the class. It hurt not to be included, but I came to expect that others would always be considered ahead of me and that would simply be my fate in this life.

Everyone who was alive then and old enough seems to remember what they were doing when John F Kennedy was shot. I was in class on that school on that day and we listened on the radio to the specifics of the assassination as they were made available. I will always remember the quiet somber mood of the class, as we listened to the reports of the event on the radio. When the president died, it seemed everyone was sad and we all watched on the TV as the horse draped in black with the boots in the stirrups turned backwards was led down the road ahead of the casket during the president’s funeral. Then little John-John saluted the casket at the end of the funeral. No one knew then that his life would end tragically at a much too early age as well.

When I signed up for the ninth grade of high school I chose college preparation courses. I didn't really believe I would ever make it to college, but it was a way of saying to others, that I might. It came to be one of the better choices I made, even though I did not as yet have the faith or courage to think I might achieve that kind of success. Being able to have a say in what I was going to study did bolster me to stretch toward making other somewhat risky choices about my life along the way. Some were beneficial and helped me mature and others were not.

Between elementary and high school, there were many times when Mother would have to call the sheriff's department and take out warrants on my Father for assault and battery. What would follow would be trips to the courthouse and courtroom. The judge would caution Daddy about his behavior, but generally that was the extent of what occurred in the courtroom.

I came to dread the trips to the courthouse, because when we were finished there, we still had to go home with Daddy. The judge was not present to deal with what happened when we got home. We knew even though Daddy had been warned it might not make a difference in what he did or said at home if and when he drank. If he thought his authority was being questioned or if he simply got angry we would all be at risk of being assaulted.

Chapter Eight
High School

When I was about 16 years old, I was with a friend in another neighborhood, and had gone with her to an evening service at Grassy Branch Church where she was a member. Bug came to the church as a visiting deacon while I was there. I noted he appeared nervous when he saw I was there. I didn't say anything to anyone about his having abused me, but I do not doubt he was concerned I might. I'm sure I had multiple fears of my own that kept me from speaking up, not the least of which was my own continuing sense of guilt for what I saw as my part in that abuse. It would be years before this misconception was addressed. By the time I was on the visit to this church I had also become a peace maker at home and tried if I could to avoid conflict in most situations.

At 16, I was also able to apply to work in the Neighborhood Youth Corp, which provided jobs for some students in some of the county high schools. I was hired shortly after I applied and I earned a small paycheck every 2 weeks. I cleaned bathrooms, swept classroom floors, cleaned and buffed the halls and sometimes straightened and cleaned the teacher's lounges. I asked to be made a teacher's aide, but those particular positions never seemed to be easily obtained and others seemed to always be picked rather than me. In looking back these positions were probably given to students who looked like they would be more likely to succeed in the business world. Regardless, I was glad for the opportunities the job offered me and it provided me a small sense of independence to have some money that I had earned from my own efforts.

This was also the time period when I met Anita Metcalf, who would be very supportive of me throughout my time in high school and while I was in the NYC. She supervised the NYC youth care students in the area. Anita expressed a measure of pride in the work I did at the school and the efforts I made toward graduating. It was appreciated. I think she might have been somewhat aware of the physical abuse that was going on at home, but not in a position to do more then be supportive and understanding of the difficulties I was experiencing.

Mother requested a small portion of each of my checks. I was not happy to have to share, but did not put up any resistance to this request. One thing that I was able to do when I received my paycheck on Friday evening's, was to cash it at a little store on the way home. I would buy a can of Sloppy Joe sauce and buns for me and the other kids to have to eat for that night's dinner. I was proud of this contribution to our meals. After cashing the check and making the purchases, I walked home (about 6 miles from where the school and store were located). These walks were my time to myself. Especially on Friday evenings when my parents were generally gone to town or the store as it was Daddy's payday as well. Mom went with him and they usually didn't get home until late, so we kids had time to ourselves that was quieter and more peaceful. If Daddy drank it was usually just a few beers before he and Mother came home and he would then often go to bed and to sleep when they got to the house.

During my last 2 years of high school, I also worked for the NYC during the summer. I was able to work more hours, so my paycheck was bigger. I also shared some of this money with my Mother, but I was able to keep larger amounts and it was enough to buy some clothes, knickknacks, and occasionally I could go to town for a movie. In addition, it afforded me a chance to have a phone extension put in the bedroom that I shared with my brothers and sister. In the beginning, Daddy was against the idea, but he grudgingly agreed when, at Mother's suggestion, I said I would pay half of the monthly phone bill. Even with brothers and sister around, it still gave me more of a measure of privacy for my phone conversations and this too helped me to feel more like what I thought a normal teenager would feel. I was even able to lay away a few items of clothing and any school supplies I might need and then I could pay for them myself.

One summer afternoon, a male I had met at the school offered to give me a ride home after work. He was tall, red headed and his eyes were somewhat crossed. Mother was visibly upset when I brought him to the house. She was probably afraid Daddy would shoot him if he saw him. After the young man left, she forbade me to ever see him again, I obeyed. Daddy had already been making statements that I would get pregnant and not finish high school. She probably thought that if he was aware this young man had driven me home and he had been alone with me in his car it would add fuel to the flame. Considering how naive I still was I can say now I am glad the young man was a gentleman and had not tried to take advantage of me.

While in the 10th grade in high school, I had made a statement in passing that I was thinking about quitting school. This seemed to startle my Mother. At that point, she decided to tell me about my parentage and my being adopted by my Step Father. I did not know of my biological father's existence until then. Mother gave me some history on his and her own relationship and said "she wouldn't have married him for a number of reasons, not the least of which was his tendency to be interested in very young women (younger than 18) and his seeming inability to make a commitment to one woman". She proceeded to warn me that I would have to take care who I dated when I was older, as he had off spring all over the area. She pointed out a picture in that session's high school yearbook of a brother I had in the same high school, and who was in the grade below mine. Mother stated his mother had been very young when she became pregnant and her family had insisted on a marriage. I often wondered if this was just mama's way of dealing with the situation. This brother was born later the same year after my birth in January of 1950. It is possible he was conceived before I was born. I never felt it was my business or place to ask so I didn't.

My next shock was that she wanted me to meet him and this family. I don't know how she got around my Step Father on this issue, but regardless, she accomplished it. Mother set the plan in motion. "Shorty" would sometimes pick me up after school and take me to this family's home for a few hours. On occasion, I would spend the night. I never thought about how the members of this family might have felt regarding my suddenly being thrust into their life until I was much older. Especially in the beginning, I was glad to be able to escape being at home where there was frequent turmoil related to my Step Fathers general behavior. I also liked being in the company of this extended family and with children closer to my age, who seemed to accept me without question. I quickly became very fond of my new family and enjoyed being able to spend time with them. My Step Mother was kind and supportive of me throughout the time I spent with them. I did see quickly that my Mother was correct and my biological father was a very flirtatious man.

Within the same time frame as my meeting my biological father and his family (and for her own various reasons) Mother also decided to tell me about the sexual abuse she experienced when she was 5 years old. She indicated a man had come to stay with her family and her mother introduced him as her "Uncle Arthur". This was during a time when Grandpa McCurry was gone from the home. He paid my Mother a lot of attention, and apparently from time to time, would tickle her until she laughed hard especially when they were alone in the house. She stated once, when they were alone, she thought he had put his thumb between her legs and pushed. She indicated she blacked out and later came to. Mother said she then realized what had physically happened and that he had molested her. She stated she had never told her mother, but thereafter she tried to avoid being around him by herself. There were many questions left unanswered related to this abuse. For a variety of my own reasons, I did not feel comfortable in broaching those questions, so they remained forever unasked and unanswered.

A numbers of years later, Mother had a chance to process on this childhood and other prominent issues, when she was required by the courts to have a psychological evaluation in relation to her having custody of my brothers and sister. This was during my parent's separation, and then divorce. Her reaction to this requirement was to be on the defensive and she stated she "did not want other people trying to change her life and who she was". She did not allow herself to take advantage of this opportunity to deal with painful and emotional issues from her past. That was a definite loss for her as a person and for all of us as a family.

When I was in the 12th grade, the NYC helped me to get set up with a dentist to treat the large number of dental problems that I was experiencing. The dentist wanted to put me in the hospital so I could go under anesthesia and he could pull the many bad teeth I had, all at once. Daddy wouldn't hear of it and refused to sign for me to be admitted to the hospital. The dentist was resistant to pull so many teeth all at once in his office, but agreed to do so when it became apparent I would not be allowed to go to the hospital. There was no question that I needed to have them removed due to the general risk they posed to my health.

A representative from the NYC agreed to take me to the appointment and then return me home when it was over. All of my upper teeth were pulled and all but 6 of the lower ones. I was then sent home with Percocet for the pain and was told to spend a few days in the bed. Once I was back at home, I was kept company by our very attentive pet squirrel Rose. On a particular day during the first week that I was recuperating, Daddy came home drinking late one evening. He was angry over some unknown cause. I was the only one at home and when he entered my room he slapped me across my face without an apparent reason. This action reopened an area on my gums where the stitches had been placed and caused the healing to be much slower.

The next time the dentist saw me he shook his head and was not very happy with this turn of events. He was required to postpone making my dentures for a number of weeks, due to the condition of my gums. This wait also resulted in my having to go to school without teeth and my senior picture was made without benefit of having an upper or lower denture. I asked one of the teachers responsible for the pictures if I could wait and do a make-up picture and she refused this request. The picture was horrid and I was always ashamed of how that senior picture looked and how it reminded me of some of the negative things that occurred during that period of my life.

It was embarrassing to be without so many teeth from a number of perspectives, not the least of which was my having to be around teachers, other students, and the public in general in what I felt was an unacceptable state. I was self-conscious and felt like there were whispers and snickers made behind my back by classmates. There is never much that can be said as a defense in such a situation. It is hard to say what was real and what was not, so I simply endured. I was very glad to finally get my dentures before graduation actually took place.

Some of my best memories from high school were my being involved in the drama club and being chosen to be the "Grinch Who Stole Christmas" during one of the Christmas plays. It was fun and I did reasonably well in the class and the role. I also enjoyed being a part of the Chorus Group. It was exciting to be able to go to different areas and schools to sing with the group and be part of some of the musical functions that took place. I at least felt like it was someplace where I could fit in. There were no questions asked within this group about home or family situations. The focus was on working together to sing the best chorus music it was possible for us to produce.

We had a music teacher who seemed to have no interest or respect of the music that was in vogue with the younger generation of the time and he would often say so. I differed with him in particular on records like “Love is Blue”. I brought him some examples of the music that was currently popular on the radio and he apparently played it sometime after that class was over.

Professor Steel never gave a verbal response of any changes in his perspective that might have developed from listening to those records. During a later school assembly, he had the band to do an impromptu presentation to the student body and he stated it was a good test of a band to be able to play music they had never seen before. The music he gave them to play was “Love is Blue”. I can say I felt almost overwhelmed and could have cried by this validation of the efforts I had made to introduce him to some of the music the students listened to at the time. I had provided him with a different view of the music that was popular with the students. His response had been to have the band play it. They did an excellent job considering they had never previously seen the musical scores although I am sure many had heard the music on the radio. I was proud of their efforts. I think the music teacher was as well. It also gave me the sense that some effort I had made did make a difference to others even if it was a small one.

I always liked the music teacher and his wife Mr. and Mrs. Steel. I later ran into her on a city street and was saddened to hear that they were asked to leave the school as instructors, due to some of their own personal beliefs. I felt like it was unfair treatment to the both of them and a major loss to the music department and student population. I told her of my sorrow for what she and her husband had experienced.

When I thought about the classes I chose to take while in high school one of the things I considered was that the classes might be good for me and might somehow be of support and be something I could share with any children I might have any in the future. Whatever prompted my choices, I am glad for the classes I picked, as they were certainly supportive of my own personal growth.

With some outside help from relatives I was grateful to be able to attend our junior and later senior proms. One of the items I had used my earnings from the NYC on was for a prom dress. I was not the "most popular girl at the ball", but that did not stop me from having a good time. At the junior prom, I was involved in presenting the evening's activities program.

I played the role of a swami, who looked into the crystal ball of the graduating class's future, and predicted wonderful things that might occur for the graduates. The dress I wore to the senior prom the next year was white and empire shaped. I was pleased to have been able to lay it away at a store and pay it out with my own money. It would come in handy for another special occasion that occurred a little later in the following year of my life after I completed high school.

Like all senior and graduating students, I sent letters of invitation out to family and friends, but my list of recipients was small. I sent one invitation to the elementary school I had attended and to the teachers that had taught me in the lower grades. I thought no more about it, until I got a card from the school, and each teacher had signed the card and put a dollar in the envelope. I was moved by this unexpected acknowledgment of my success. I've never forgotten how important that experience was to me and how appropriate it can be to acknowledge others contribution to the successes I have experienced in my life.

I hadn't dated at all until my senior year and then had one triple date, setup by a concerned girlfriend and classmate of mine.

As a group, we went to a drive-in movie. I felt self-conscious and out of my element the whole time we were there, and after the date was over, I never heard from the fellow again. I appreciated the invitation and my friends attempt to include me in what was probably for her an ordinary outing but what was for me at that point a once in a lifetime experience.

I attended my first and only high school football game my senior year. It was the final one of the season and my biological father had taken me and some of my siblings to watch the game. The only school dance I ever attended was the one that was held the night after we graduated from high school. Mrs. Whitney a friend of mothers had taken us to the graduation. She dropped me off at the dance, after one of the other students agreed to give me a ride home when the dance was over. I sincerely appreciated that consideration and it is one of my fondest memories from my high school years.

The last year of high school, the students around me were busy making plans for their future. I had none and had no idea what I wanted to do. Since I apparently needed something to plan on before graduation, I decided to take a test with the local army reserve. I scored high in a couple of areas, but due to my being 18, I would have needed my parent's consent to go into the service.

My parents, especially Daddy, would not agree to sign for me to join, which put an end to those potential plans. I didn't even consider that I could go in on my own when I was a little older. I was too impulsive to wait the number of years it would take for me to make those steps into the service. That could have certainly taken my life in a different direction.

Chapter Nine
Employment

The summer after graduation, I got a job at the local hosiery mill. I knew I needed some kind of a job, it was walking distance from my home, and the income would give me a larger sense of freedom than I had previously experienced. I quickly found I was not cut out to be a good mill worker, as I was slow at the sewing and also somewhat uncoordinated in the process. I worked at this job for a little over a month and then started looking for something different. It was interesting that after I had resigned from the factory I then received a pink slip along with a number of other employees. I would have been laid off soon so it was good I had already chosen to leave.

I saw an advertisement in the Asheville newspaper for a Nurse's Aide position at a local mental health hospital. The advertisement indicated the facility would train the applicants. It was located on the local bus line and it looked like a job I might be able to do. My perception of the job ran the gamut of my imagination, and I visualized myself being seated beside a patient who was tied to the bed in which he was sleeping. When he was awake I was reading to him, while a male technician or an officer of sorts was sitting outside the door of the room. This was in case he was needed for some emergency assistance. This perception was a lot different than the reality, but like most people, I had only movies I had seen, stories I had heard and my imagination to go by.

I applied for the position and had an interview with Marge Johnson, the Director of Nursing at Highlands Hospital a short time later. I think she may have had a number of reservations about hiring me. She may also have seen some of the potential that I possessed. She did hire me, and I was off on a on a new phase of my life.

Mrs. Johnson would come to be my first real role model in nursing and I think of her often, even after all these years. Her strength was personal and internal. It was what she brought to the job, not what the jobs title gave to her. Later after I became a nurse I was working on a floor with her. I was then able to tell her of my appreciation of her strength and support that she provided to me, and the effect it had on me up to that point in my life. She retired a short time after that conversation and left employment at this hospital.

The job was not at all what I imagined it to be. It was

interesting, educational and in many ways satisfying, in the sense of learning new skills and providing support to others. At the time, I was still very green behind the gills and had a very lot to learn about life. I was in numerous and varied classes during the orientation to job responsibilities and quickly developed a more realistic view of a Nurses Aides' responsibilities. I enjoyed the classes, for the sake of the learning in and of itself. This was certainly a different kind of learning then what I had experienced in school. This was an education about life and ways to provide healthy support.

The clients often had outside activities with staff, like exercising and playing volleyball or softball, and I was able to take part in these activities as well. In the evening on the units, we also were able to play cards and table games with the clients, as it provided them with interaction and socialization. One of the responsibilities we had as aides was to assist other staff in placing out of control clients in restrictive holds and restraints. In the beginning, this was a strange and exciting experience for me. It was a more physical and formalized way to be able to help control another person's anger and outburst. Coming from an abused childhood, I can understand how that might have been my initial perception and reaction in response to clients who were aggressive.

Over the years and as I matured, I found that it was not a healthy reaction to feel good about physically restraining anyone in order to make them do what was wanted. I thankfully matured, and have since purposefully tried to learn nonphysical ways to deal with highly charged situations. It is not good for the client under my care to use restraints or restrictive holds if it can be avoided and it was certainly not good for me. I was glad for all involved when I gained that broader insight and perspective.

During the first few weeks I worked at this hospital, I met a guard who monitored the buildings and the grounds of the facility, along with other rounds he made in various areas of Asheville. After a few days of general conversations, he offered to give me a ride home. This occurred a few times and then he started picking me up in the mornings to bring me in to work. I was flattered by his attentions and his apparent concerns about me. I was not used to any male paying me this kind of attention and naive about his intentions and any expectations he might have of me.

One afternoon, when he was taking me home, he detoured to a wooded and secluded area close to a creek. The relationship progressed to a physical state where I was “in over my head”, creating a situation where he firmly "pushed” me into the physical act of intercourse. It hurt and even though I had been molested as a child, I still bled as a result of the incident. I was very upset and tearful when he later dropped me off at home.

No one else was home, for which I was grateful. I can remember quickly bathing and throwing the underclothes away. I vowed to myself I wouldn't see him again, but I was already in a pattern of having minimal expectations in a relationship and had developed little self-esteem and no particular sense of boundaries. Had he called, I know now I would have gone with him without question.

The next day, I was off from work and I placed a call to the dispatcher of the guards company. I asked to have the guard call me. I was told his wife had asked that no messages from females other than herself be relayed to her husband through the dispatcher. When I got off the phone, I was shocked, hurt, angry and humiliated. It was the first time I had ever thought about the possibility of suicide. It was a transient thought, but there, none the less.

I did not continue the relationship, which was a positive. It would have been a plus for me if I had continued to recognize what defined positive choices in my life. I still had much to learn. I had not consciously connected that I had a responsibility in the kind of negative decisions I was making or the risky and potentially dangerous situations in which my negative decisions could place me.

I sit in the corner of my circular room
and watch the snow as the rain comes down
I ponder the points to my rounded table
and I dream as time passed me by

Chapter Ten
Bill and Our Years Together

One morning, a few weeks after the incident with the guard, I was taking the clients to breakfast from the floor on which I worked. I met a young man and his cousin walking down a breezeway of the facility. They were dressed in kitchen work cloths, and in conversation stated they worked in the main kitchen of the hospital. Bill was young, full of life, redheaded and sweet.

After a number of days and conversations, he asked me out. With his continued encouragement and attention, I became interested in his offer of a date. I did make sure he was single and had never been married. My father overheard me say I was going to date someone who worked at the hospital with me and he forbade me to do so. Daddy was not aware of the situation that had occurred with the guard and I had no intentions of enlightening him. Being told I could not date someone became a motivator for me. I realized it was probably time for me to move out. I felt a little guilty for leaving Mama and my siblings alone with Daddy, but the need to be my own boss in relation to seeing others and being out on my own proved to be the stronger drive.

I found an available room at a house just at the end of the hospital road. By being closer to the hospital I could sleep later in the morning. This was an affordable room, it was comfortable, I did not have to have my own furniture and I would not have far to walk to get to the unit on which I worked. I would not have to worry about transportation as I would now be living close to the workplace and I could ride the city bus if I wanted to go to town. I would also be away from the constant strain and dysfunctional dynamics that were still taking place at home. I could then date whomever I wanted. Once I completed the move I was able to refocus on Bills offer of a date.

I immediately enjoyed the peace and quiet of my own space. Once I was situated Bill and I began to go out and spend time together. He didn't make any untoward advances and seemed a little shy and innocent, which I found attractive. We dated several weeks before our relationship moved into a more physical phase. He then asked me to marry him and my immediate response was "yes". I asked myself "wasn't that what women were supposed to do"? I felt lucky to have even been asked, especially after the situation that had occurred with the guard. I did not understand terms like independence, self-esteem, or the characteristics of a healthy relationship. The Director of Nursing at the hospital tried to talk to me about the choice I was making, but I was unwilling to hear what she was trying to tell me. I was too immature and impulsive to make a balanced judgment so we continued with our plans to marry.

We were married within a few months. My natural father and his wife helped to set up the wedding and one of my classmates from high school agreed to be my maid of honor. It was a pretty wedding and we had taken the white dress I had worn to my senior prom and converted it into a wedding dress. A few months after we were married, I became pregnant. I was nineteen and we had been married 10 months, when I gave birth to our first son William.

During our first year together, and shortly after William's birth, a situation occurred where Mother and my siblings were brought to my aunt's house that was located just up the street from where we lived. Daddy had beaten Mother badly. The Sheriff's department took the children and Mother to the hospital and from there to my aunt's house. The next day, they came to our tiny one bedroom apartment to stay for a few days. Mother slept in a recliner and my brothers and sister slept tightly packed together on the couch.

Apparently my parents had just borrowed a moderate sum

of money from a loan company and mother had it in her possession. With this money in hand, she saw it as the time to separate from my Step Father. While Mama was still gone from the home, he moved from the house and temporarily stayed with his mother. Mama and my siblings were then able to go back home. She took out a restraining order on him and then took him to court. As far as I know he never attempted to hit mama again. They filed separation papers and then were later divorced. I was never quite sure how but he managed to avoid giving her alimony. He must have hired a good lawyer. He then moved in with, and later married the lady next door. Mother had suspected they had been having an affair long before she and Henry separated. His moving in with her so quick after the separation gave some support to this suspicion.

There would follow, for Mother, many trips to court and battles over child support. Mama was disappointed that she was never able to get any alimony out of the situation, but she did receive a small amount of child support for each child until each became older and was considered an adult. With the courts encouragement Father did finish paying for the home place. My youngest brother, as a child was found to be mentally retarded and developmentally disabled. Some of my parent's biggest battles over money turned out to be due to this brothers needs for continued care at home.

Mother and this brother were eventually able to receive disability payments in addition to Medicaid coverage for medical needs. Daddy's marriage to the neighbor did not last very long, as Daddy began to beat her as well. She, at one point, apologized to Mother for having associated with Henry and then having married him and for any trouble their relationship might have caused Mother.

Not long after Daddy left the home, Mama developed and then over time more openly presented with patterns of hoarding. Thereafter, she was often visited by representatives of the city and health department. As the years went by her sisters, I and later my younger sister, tried to save Mother from herself. The harder we tried, the less we seemed to succeed. We came to realize it was an unrealistic goal as each time the home was cleared of clutter Mother would then start to hoard again. This practice would eventually lead to the house being condemned, but that was much further into the future.

My husband Bills family had a number of mental health challenges of their own that included his father being a long time alcoholic. Bills dad developed dementia secondary to his alcoholism not too long after Bill and I married. At one point Bill's dad drank wood alcohol which placed him in the hospital and led to his being sent to a nursing home.

Bills mother Hazel was a simple country woman with minimal education. When our first son William was born, Hazel lived in a house with her daughter, 4 young grandchildren, and her own mother. Over our first few years together, Bill and I spent a lot of time at Hazels home. We used buses for transportation and due to work often needed a baby sitter, so his mother became our first choice. She would keep William for a number of days at a time and then we would have him on our days off. I was not happy with this extended arrangement, as I wanted our son to be at home with us as much as possible.

My mother-in-law heated with a wood stove and on two separate occasions when William was small and in her care, he got burned on the same spot on his arm by having his arm touch the wood stove. I never knew exactly how it happened but I was furious that it did and I demanded things would have to change. That is when Bill made moves to obtain his driver's license, and for us to purchase a car. We could then find a baby sitter closer to home and be able to pick William up when we finished work in the evenings.

Bill changed jobs a number of times throughout our first few years together. When William was about 3 years old, Bill had employment in the housekeeping department at Mission Hospital. At around this time, Bills mom and grandmother became homeless and moved into our apartment with us. I think due to this event and life in general I became depressed and experienced a false pregnancy. We thought maybe if I had another child it might help how I was feeling. We both thought that perhaps the absence of a young baby in the home was part of the problem I was experiencing. I was again too naive to look beyond the moment. I became pregnant a short time later.

While I was carrying our second child, we decided 2 children would be enough and we signed papers that I would have my tubes tied after this second child was born. I did not recognize the seriousness or intensity of my depressive feelings until after I had given birth to our second son John. When he was born, I had begun to question if I really wanted to have my tubes tied, as I had been convinced he would be a girl. This was an issue I never really got to consider or deal with prior to and after his birth.

I went into labor early one morning and was admitted to the hospital maternity ward. My blood pressure became elevated during and after John's delivery to a level that placed my health at risk. The Obstetrician ordered medications that kept me somewhat sedated for a number of hours. I never had another opportunity to explore my then identified concerns about surgical sterilization and was taken to surgery early the next morning to have my tubes cut and tied.

From surgery, I was taken to the recovery room, and I woke to find Bill smacking me on my face. I was startled and angry in reaction. I guessed the nurses there felt like it would be all right since he worked at the hospital, to be in with me, but it made for me a very negative and unsettling experience and I carried that frustration and anger over the situation in my memory for many years.

After I got home, I continued to feel depressed and I called the obstetrician about my concerns. He indicated I was probably going through a postpartum depression. All I knew was that I was not happy and I cried a lot. There was no consideration made by the physician that I might have benefited from antidepressants. It is possible this intervention could have made a difference for me and how I generally felt. This was prior to a time when antidepressants were used on a more frequent basis as a treatment for this type of depression.

Bills grandmother died shortly after John was born and with

the obstetrician's blessings, I did not attend the funeral. Bills sister and her children came over to our home to go with Bill and his mother to the funeral. One of her sons had on one of Williams new shirts. Bills sister had apparently taken it while visiting at our home, during the time I was in the hospital delivering John. I was irritated and frustrated at this taking of his clothes without my permission. I had no support from Bill when I brought up the issue. What might have otherwise been considered as a simple loan of a child's shirt to another child took on much larger dimensions then it might have if I had not been experiencing such an intense state of depression.

I returned to work when John was 3 months old. I still tried to breastfeed him for a time even after going back to work. Within a few months I developed a kidney infection and had to change John over to a regular bottle, due to the potential that the antibiotic could be passed on to him through the breast milk. With this loss of a last link to childbirth my depression intensified.

The symptoms didn't really start to abate until John was about 15 months old. This was when I had really begun to look at my life, mine and Bills life together, and my need to be a different person. Toward the end of the marriage and after I had obtained my driver's license, I began to recognize the value of making my own decisions. As I continued to process and explore my situation, I realized a number of truths. I wanted to grow into more than I was at that time and felt I could not do that while in the marriage. In spite of problems at home, I was doing well in the work setting. I even had a psychiatrist and a social worker who worked at the hospital to make an offer to me of being a personal reference, should I ever decide to return to school. That became definite food for thought and initiative for growth within the months and years ahead.

Throughout our lives together, Bill had resisted any attempts I had made toward change even though I had been supportive of him in his own attempts toward growth. He seemed to feel threatened by my wanting to go back to school. He had already tried to control me in a number of other ways that had included my choices in clothing. One particular incident related to my choice in clothes was a V neck dress that I sometimes wore. Bill would often complain it “revealed too much”. He convinced me to buy another outfit in exchange for it. He then took the dress and burned it in front of me. I thereafter regretted making that choice. He attempted to put more controls on other decision’s I made and activities in which I participated. On one occasion he even sought to stop me from voting in the local and presidential elections. I was irate and after an intense argument, went to the poles and voted anyway. I had also begun to realize that perhaps I was not in love with Bill anymore and wondered if I ever had been.

On an occasion a few months later, Bill agreed to take a friend of his to a town in the eastern part of the state. The friend had no license or vehicle. When he returned from the trip, he told me he had been indiscreet with another woman. This undermined whatever trust I had left in him and the marriage seemed to deteriorate after this incident. Then his supervisor at the hospital where he was employed decided to put him on the night shift and I thereby got use to sleeping alone. I began having intense nightmares, one of which was my need to have surgery for the removal of a diseased organ. Our dreams can often reflect our waking conflicts and thoughts and I am sure this was a mirrored image of the changes in life I felt I needed and wanted to make.

I was still insecure about making major decisions and before I made any actual moves to leave, I considered that Bill and I should go in for a counseling session. Bill agreed to go, so I made an appointment for us at the local mental health center. I wanted to be sure that, on my part, I had tried all that I thought I should have to make the marriage work. I needed to see if an outside, unbiased observer could understand my concerns and hear what was being said by the both of us. She or he could then give us some feedback.

When we went to the appointment, we were seen by a female clinician. At the end of the session the counselor made the observation that I seemed to view things more from a grey area and my husband was a more black and white thinker. Things for him were all one way or another, with nothing in-between. He was happy with things the way they were and did not want anything to change. I couldn't continue like I had been in the situation and had a definite need to be different.

The counselor offered to meet with me in individual appointments if I felt I needed them, but I wasn't yet ready to identify and tackle bigger issues. In looking back over our years together, I was glad we had each made a number of milestones in our lives. He had obtained his driver's license, which gave him a measure of independence. He had kept a good job for a number of years and he was a caring father. I had my driver's license, a desire to be something different, and a need to further my education.

Chapter Eleven
Life after Our Separation

Bill initially agreed to provide child support for the children and I did not ask for alimony for myself. We separated, and I told him to take anything in the house he wanted. We really had little to divide. After the separation, I bought my first car, a 1962 Chevy Bel-Air that had been advertised in the area where I lived. The owner had initially wanted $50.00 for it and I was pleased with that price. When I had someone to take me to pick up the car, the seller said he knew I would "have to buy a battery for it" and only charged me $35.00 to purchase the car. Mother later bought the battery, which cost more than the car at $40.00. I loved that old car, wing tips and all. It served me well for the next couple of years and having this source of transportation gave me an independence I had not experienced prior to owning my own car.

After Bill and I separated he and I had a number of verbal altercations especially during that first year apart. On occasions, when I went to various locations, I would find he was following me. This practice was a partial cause of John falling and breaking out a baby tooth, when Bill showed up of a sudden at a local McDonald's. A friend had taken the kids and I out for a burger. Lee and I had known each other since childhood and we both worked at the same hospital. I presume Bill saw him as a romantic interest, which at that time he wasn't. Bill drove past the glass window of the McDonald's at a fast rate, which rattled the building and John fell from the place he had been seated in his car seat. Johns fall resulted in his needing some oral treatment for the broken tooth.

The year we separated we filed taxes together. Bill met me at the bank when the check came in so we could cash it. He slapped me when he felt like he had not gotten his fair share of the check. I went to the lawyer that was handling the separation about this incident and he sent Bill a rather sharp letter related to things that could occur if he was ever physically abusive to me again. The situation was never repeated.

After this incident, things settled into more of a routine. He paid child support of $10 per child a week, we established visitation times with the children, and we got on with life. That arrangement lasted with only minimal problems, for a couple of years. Bill was then involved in a serious automobile accident in which he had been intoxicated, and this was a part of the cause of his wreck. He was not able to work for several months and therefore not able to pay child support. I accepted this without complaint for a time. It became difficult to provide the children with some of the things they needed, but I waited until after he recovered and went back to work to ask him about the support. He was still resistant to catching up on the payments and stated he just could not do so. He indicated that the credit union would not make him a loan. I told him just not to bother as I would raise the kids by myself and without his support. He never paid child support to me again and for many years did not visit with the children on a regular basis.

After we had been separated for several months, I would occasionally go out with some of my coworkers. After work we would sometimes go to a restaurant and get something to eat or we might go to someone's house to unwind. It was during those outings that I found myself among others who used a variety of recreational drugs. I was hesitant in regards to drugs and it didn't take me long to realize this kind of activity, in addition to being illegal, could lead someone like me into addiction. Fear can be a good thing sometimes. That fear of addiction I then carried probably kept me from getting caught up in drugs that could have taken over and destroyed my life. If I went out with a group of coworkers I would generally drink lightly, and sometimes not at all. I was amazed at how broadly available drugs were in the community and how many of the people I knew participated in using them. I thought maybe I was just naive about much of the world around me. I wanted to be accepted by others, but I generally tried to stay clear of situations where I could get into trouble.

Chapter Twelve
Bobby

In the spring of 1975, I set about finding the children and myself a smaller apartment. I dated Lee a few more times and he helped us to make that move. Lee and I parted ways in an amicable fashion. Within the following year, I considered my options of going back to school. The first step was to take a job aptitude and placement test at the local employment security commission. I scheduled and took that test within the next few months. As I was already a Nurse's Aide, it made sense to me to consider going into nursing school. I had been encouraged by nurses, social workers and physicians around me to make some initial steps toward returning to school. I admired the nurses I worked with and felt like they made a difference in the lives of the clients they provided services for and all of the lives they touched.

When I had taken the job aptitude placement test, the scores I made indicated I should be able to pass Practical Nurses Education classes without difficulty. If I chose the Associate Degree Nurses program, it would be much more intense and I might not as yet be able to pass that program. I decided I would try for the PNE program, so I could get back into the work setting as quickly as possible. It would take only a year to take all the classes and sit for the exam.

Prior to taking any steps toward applying for technical college, Mother introduced me to a man she had recently met and thought I might like to date. At her encouragement, I called him and shortly thereafter we began to go out together. In early 1976, we had decided to move in together. I rented a house from the same landlord from whom I had rented an apartment. Then Bobby, the kids, and I moved to this new location on State Street in West Asheville.

I made the initial inquires about how to get into the nursing program and did some independent study in the learning lab at Asheville Buncombe Technical College. I wanted to get reacquainted with the idea of studying and taking tests. I felt it was a good move. When I took that entrance exam I did much better than I probably would have otherwise done. I passed with high scores, especially in reading comprehension, and then I requested admission into the nursing program. After sending in my references, I was scheduled for an interview. Meanwhile, I was very caught up in many aspects of my new relationship and although I was not consciously aware of it, I was becoming increasingly dependent on Bobby in a variety of ways.

It was foolish, and unreal, the kind of situations and the stresses I began to put myself through, all in the name of "having a boyfriend" or "someone to take care of" who would in turn would "take care of me". The longer I was with Bobby, the less able I seemed to be without him. He was almost like a narcotic I could not stay away from. I realized later a part of that attraction was because the physical relationship was intense and satisfying. In my perception this was the non-verbal definition of love and what was supposed to be achieved in a relationship.

Bobby encouraged me to be involved with smoking, drinking, and partying with his friends. He voiced a much more liberal attitude toward relationships with others than I held. This caused me a lot of confusion and created a lot of friction between us especially when he would push the limits of what behaviors I would and would not accept out of him. He seemed to keep upping the ante in the games that he would play and I seemed to keep loosening the boundaries of what I would accept and allow.

I developed insomnia and got into the habit of smoking material Bobby had available, in order to get to sleep. It reached a point where I had been smoking every night for three months and it was a major shock to me when I came to that realization. I stopped cold turkey and then knew at least a little of what it was like to crave a substance. It took me three weeks to get into a regular sleep pattern. I realized again, it would be easy for me to become addicted to substances and it was an added lesson to which I tried to pay attention.

Chapter Thirteen
Practical Nurses Education Classes

I was accepted into the PNE program and started classes in the fall of 1976. I applied for and received a number of grants that would help me pay for my fees, books and uniforms. During that time period, I can remember strong disagreements I was having with Bobby on a variety of issues. When I went for an appointment with a newspaper and representative from the scholarship committee for publicity pictures in support of the scholarship I had received, I had been crying intensely as a result of the arguments. I used a lot of heavy make-up to try and cover the evidence. The pictures reflected the heavy make-up I had applied.

I was determined to attend the PNE classes and become an LPN regardless of what occurred between Bobby and I. That determination would help me in a number of areas of my life, when the time came for me to make some needed changes and to take a number of important steps forward.

I thought about the many nurses who were role models for me. Many encouraged me to go further with my education and improve my life situation. The numerous nurses I worked with all had different personalities, different ways of approaching a crises, different ways of looking at life and a wealth of experience to draw from when psychiatric emergencies arose. The main element they shared in common was the consistency with which they cared for and about the clients in our facility.

We had nursing students who did a rotation through our facility. While these students were there for classes I met one of the first nursing instructors I would come to know and appreciate. Mable Carlyle was a single mom and a Western Carolina University Nursing graduate and instructor. She brought several students to Highlands Hospital for their Mental Health clinical rotation. I admired her determination and ability to succeed by completing nursing school and becoming a nurse while raising her children.

I liked her knowledge of nursing and life, her bright smile, and her witty ways. She was one of the first nurses who encouraged me to consider going back to school. Mable would be a firm supporter and mentor over the years, while I traveled the course of my life and education. I have always been honored and pleased to call her friend. Our paths would cross often, especially when I later returned to school at Western for my Bachelor of

Science in Nursing Degree.

It amazed me at times how many people around me seem to have faith in what I might be able to accomplish, long before I had that hope or belief for myself. When coworkers found out I was considering returning to school, some would offer their support and many indicated they would be glad to be used as a reference. I remembered these encouragements as I returned to school, and especially when classes and schedules got hectic, difficult and almost overwhelming.

When the nursing classes started, I was again excited about learning and enjoyed being in an educational situation with others who had similar interest to my own. I liked my teachers and felt like this was something I could learn. I would be able to succeed as a Licensed Practical Nurse.

I remember the names of some of my first instructors; Brenda Causey, Linda Holder, Ms Norwicki, Mrs. Gouge, and Bonnie Saylor were some of the teachers I knew. One of the things I recall was when Ms Norwicki, who was a short stout woman, tested her students metal by using somewhat confrontational questioning to see if they would be able to stand up to the stresses of nursing. She tended to attempt to weed out the students who would not have the strength or stamina to make a good nurse.

Mrs. Saylor was a tall (tallest of the teachers there) broad shouldered, dark haired woman with a wonderful sense of humor and a firm understanding of the nursing and life information she wanted us to learn. Mrs. Causey was a young, bright nurse with intense eyes and a definite interest in her students and the clients for whom they provided care. She became a mother during her time as an educator in the nursing program. Mrs. Holder was firm, solid and knowledgeable about what she taught and she was patient with the students in her classes. Mrs. Gouge was pleasant, a good teacher and was being courted while we were her students.

The first person I was assigned to take care of on our first clinical day on one of the clinical floors of the hospital died during the time I was giving her a bath. Her breathing had been very slow to begin with, so it was difficult for me to tell if her breaths had totally ceased. Unsure, but suspecting that was the case, I sought Mrs. Saylor out immediately. This client was a woman who was listed as a no code, and after checking her breathing, Mrs. Saylor motioned me out of the room. She notified the floor charge nurse of this occurrence. Established protocol was then followed. One of my biggest anxieties at that time had been what would be said to the family and at what point. I would have thought the family would have been told immediately and did not realize there was an established process that needed to take place first.

Mrs. Saylor counseled me later in the shift, than we discussed the experience as a class the next time we met. Mrs. Saylor unexpectedly died a few years later and I was able to attend her funeral. I was saddened for her children, for the loss of their mother, and for the nursing profession for the loss of a good instructor and dedicated nurse.

For every grey and dusky morn
You will find a patch of blue
For every time I need a friend
I hope to find someone like you

An interesting side note to my completing that PNE class occurred when pictures were made for the AB tech year book that year. Mine came out in the Associate Degree of Nursing portion of the book rather than the Practical Nursing in Education section. It might have been a portent of things yet to come.

Sometimes we look at those around us later in life and consider where they were at in parallel to ourselves earlier in life. This was true with a young man who shared a space and time with me when I was in Practical Nurse Education classes. A slender, young black male, who was taking his first steps into the field of nursing was in this program with me. He was a good student and likeable person, who later climbed his way up the nursing ladder, to become president of the North Carolina Nurses Association and a board member of the American Nurses Association as well.

Ernie Grant was always a charmer, even in those early days of his nursing education and always a caring person. He took steps in a profession that was at the time generally filled with women and rarely shared by men especially of color. He has let his steps take him far and wide up the ladder of success in his nursing career. I was very pleased a few years later, in my own career to see him at various nursing functions. He had matured well and became a wonderful role model for others to follow. Ernie has become a gentle giant of a man, with a heart to match his height. It has been such a pleasure to watch his growth and to also have been able to tell him how much I admired his dedication to his chosen profession. He is a definite role model to other nurses and a wonderful support to those patients who are under his care.

One of the scholarships I received when I had first started back to school was from the National Association of Practical Nurses Education Association. It had never been given locally. In addition to having my picture placed in the local newspaper, I was later able to attend a PNE nursing conference with other students in the area. This conference was my first introduction to a nursing association and it left a very positive impression. Since I had won the scholarship, I was able to take part in the opening ceremony of the conference. I was excited and pleased about that experience.

When I first became a student I had borrowed money from the North Carolina College Foundation and put it into a savings account, against the variety of potential school needs I would have to address. Bobby had a job with a welding company and I had a number of grants and scholarships on hand when school started. When we moved in together Bobby and I pooled our resources and managed pretty well. I was still somewhat naïve and expected far too much from this relationship. I also did not know, until much later, that he had promised my mother he would stay with me, at least until I completed the PNE program. When I completed my classes, I still had most of the money in the bank from my loan. Bobby wanted me to go to work at a McDonald's until I took my state boards and received the results which could provide me with my license to practice as a nurse. My feelings were hurt and I was insulted by his suggestion. I felt like I needed to be working in the medical field. I sought out a job working for a nurse's registry as a nurse's aide which would at least keep me in an area of patient care and make my transition into nursing a little easier.

Bobby decided to quit the job he had at a welding company and he asked me to use the borrowed money I had saved in the bank to start a small business. I was hesitant, but had not recognized the need nor developed needed boundaries to be able to say no. I let him use the money to lease a small store and minor automotive repair business that he established with one of his somewhat liberal friends. The numbers and intensity of our arguments increased.

I was also very suspicious he was seeing someone else. I had found another woman's scarf and sunglasses in Bobby's dune buggy along with a bag that contained a couple of full beer cans in it. I knew the scarf and sunglasses were certainly not mine and that Bobby did not like nor did he drink beer. When I talked with my mother about what I found she expressed concern that in addition to his possibly being untrue that I might lose the money I loaned him as he might not pay it back. I would then not have it to give back when the school loan was due to be repaid a short time later. She counseled me to be cautious and suggested I might even want to have him followed. With her suggestion in mind I hired a private detective, and found out within 2 days he was indeed seeing another woman. I wanted to catch him red handed so one evening I went unannounced to the new business he and his friend had opened. This woman arrived shortly after I got there, as he had no way to warn her off.

The scene was not pretty and I was irate, but as I still continued to do what I was told I left the business when Bobby insisted I do so. I found out much later he had, in fact, had the woman in our home during times when I was gone from the house and when I was at work.

After the scene at the new business, he stopped trying to keep this affair private. He would simply go to see her when he took a notion. I found out where she lived, what her phone number was, what she drove, and where she worked. She apparently passed our house each evening when she got off from work, and I became obsessed with watching for her to go by in the evening. I even nicknamed her Darth Vader due to her having dark hair and dark glasses perched upon her nose. One particular night I felt desperate and called her house to beg Bobby to come home. His answer was to say only if he could bring her with him. That statement from him should have ended our relationship but it didn't. I was still too caught up in this cycle of abuse and my unrealistic need to have this man in my life.

If we had simply parted ways and I had made a clean break, it would have been the best response to the situation and a sign of my being more mature. To say I felt shame and was demoralized is to put it mildly. From this acceptance of his actions and attitude, I spiraled downward until I hit an emotional bottom. I was constantly frustrated and unhappy, because I couldn't make this relationship into what I wanted it to be. I thought I had to succeed in keeping him in my life, or I would be a failure. This was regardless of the emotional cost that I had to pay. I could not acknowledge this challenge to our relationship, or to my own false belief in what this relationship meant. I used denial and fought so hard to maintain the existence of my own view of this ideal life with Bobby which was built on false hopes and physical parameters. I could not see there would never be a chance for this relationship to be healthy or successful.

Late fall of that year, I told Bobby if he was going to be with me, he needed to make it a permanent stay, with rings and commitment. A part of me knew he could not take this step and it would force him to some sort of choice. I had finally drawn a line. He left, and although he would sometimes come back to "visit" and, on occasion "want to stay a day or so" it was generally over. I saw him less and less over the next year, without missing him as much as I had at the beginning of the separation. He did eventually, and with encouragement, pay the money back to me that I had loaned him. I was than able to repay the loan when it came due. I was relieved by having the money back in hand and being able to pay off this debt in a timely fashion.

I received the results of my state boards a short time later and I had passed. I was now a Licensed Practical Nurse. At least I had gained a little more security for myself and could better provide for my children's future, regardless of what occurred within the relationship with Bobby. I started to work in a state sponsored position at the Tuberculosis Sanitarium in Black Mountain NC, in the fall of 1977.

I had been employed at the Sanatorium for a few months when I had a worsening of a medical condition that would require I have a hysterectomy that December. I had little sick leave and it looked to be a very sparse Christmas, especially for the children. Brenda Smith, one of the nurses I knew at work, did a drive at work to help us, and pulled the staff together to provide Christmas for me and my children. When I protested that it was too much to ask of others, this nurse reminded me that it is sometimes important for others to have an opportunity to help their fellow man. She encouraged me to just say thank you and let this process happen.

I have since come to understand the lesson that she meant. We met again many years later, when she was a nurse educator who brought students to another facility where I worked, for their clinical rotation. She was in fact the nurse who encouraged me to become a clinical nurse myself. She did not remember the kind deed she had done for me and my children so many years before, but I certainly did.

After I recovered from surgery and returned to work, I gained my first experience as an actual nurse. I saw people die with dignity from cancer and other respiratory ailments. I learned that sometimes when a patient is dying from lung cancer, he may still want that last cigarette minutes before his final breath is taken, that you can become attached to a patient and be supportive of his or her needs when he or she crosses through deaths door.

That attachment for me would later translate into a more helpful empathy. I learned you can become humble in the presence of a families faith and anguish, the importance of supporting each other, staff and patients, as fellow humans, and that life and death will happen in its own time and order. We each do our best to prepare for those changes, as they occur. I learned as much about myself as I did those around me.

Some of the feelings I became aware of, were that I was terrified of the idea of my own mortality and that at times I experienced intense and high levels of anxiety. That was as far at the time as I got toward identifying my own mental health issues. My fears around death at one point became so intense that I put myself through a mental scenario of dying, in order to try to get past this immobilizing fear. This visualization seemed to help to decrease this fears hold over me.

After Bobby moved out and a number of months after I had recovered from my surgery, I started going out with girl friends of mine that worked at the TB hospital. We would go to a local club where there was a live band and people were able to dance. I would feed the boys supper and then leave them watching television. These were times when they were alone and responsible for themselves.

With hindsight, I can say it was not the good idea I thought it was at the time. Based on how I was raised, I can now see that it was not a healthy practice. At the time, I had convinced myself it would foster independence for the children. It later instead seemed to help create resentment, especially from my oldest son. The boys at that time were 9 and 5 years of age.

The wings of night softly flutter to the ground
And close the door to the sun
And heavy eyelids drag me down
To sleep
To dream
Of lazy ivy
And stonewalled castles in the sky

During one of these nights out with my friends, I ran into Jimmy. He had been in two grades above me in the elementary and high schools we both attended. Jimmy was someone I was familiar with and with whom I had a connection from the past. He was nice, generally settled, and my impression was that he had been separated from his first wife for a number of months. He had three beautiful kids, two sons and a daughter, who were close to my son's ages.

Jimmy had the responsibility of all of his children in his care. He was a single parent like I was and I appreciated and respected his willingness to raise his children on his own. We started dating. Ours was a pleasant relationship and had the potential to develop into something more positive and long term than ones I had known in the past. The kids all enjoyed playing together and got along well. We dated several months in general harmony. Jimmy was fun to be with, he had a natural rhythm about him, and he was a wonderful dancer. His smile was sweet and I loved to look in his beautiful eyes.

I got frightened one evening when he started telling me of dreams he was having, where we were together all the time. I was afraid of what this unspoken statement might mean and I felt I would not be able to handle the commitment this relationship might have required, so I pulled away from Jimmy.

That was probably the healthiest friendship I had experienced, up to that point in time and in my life. I was just not mature enough to take the steps that might have been required of me to become more mature in the relationship. I later missed his kids almost as much as I missed his company and companionship, but I just could not get past the fears of what that we might become ad what that commitment might mean to us both. That was over twenty five years ago.

Gently touch my body
Love me with your mind
Winters soon a coming
And will leave us far behind
We're now and softly fading
Walking to the Past
The warmth is here forever
Caring to the last

I ran into him recently at a grocery store and we talked for a long time. I told him I was sorry I had broken off with him so suddenly. I explained that it was nothing he had done, that it had been my own fears and insecurities that had brought about my part of ending the relationship. He said he had always wondered and was glad to know what had happened and that it was not his fault I had left. His children are grown and he has grandchildren of his own. He is a kind soul and I hope for him to have the best that life has to offer.

This simple encounter gave me a chance to gain some peace on an area of my life where I had felt anguish and guilt. I was able to acknowledge to another person the positive feelings I had felt for him and I was grateful for that opportunity. I think he was as well. When we parted, he came out to where I was parked, to again say goodbye. That extra effort on his part left a warm spot in my heart that I would remember later when my life again turned upside down.

Jimmy is a Veteran of the Vietnam War. At a point later in our lives when we were older we again became acquainted and shared a friendship. I wrote the following poem in response to the pain from war that I sometimes sensed in this compassionate and caring man. In his own way he has taught me so much about life and I am grateful for those lessons. I am honored to call him friend.

Veteran of a Foreign War

High school just over and graduation behind me
What to do now
with this new life ahead
War across the ocean
Quietly whispers in my ears
that I must go in the footsteps of others
Could anything I thought or dreamed prepare me
For the fears and horrors
Of the real life and death waiting there
Anger and anguish in equal amounts
Weighed heavy upon my mind and shoulders and soul
there was no sense of safety as each day began
Caution was required not to think too deep
To care too much or bond too closely with anyone
There were never any guarantees of a tomorrow
To acknowledge such intense pain and agony
was just too much to accept
to expect or deal with
I know I am among those who fought,
stood tall and survived
the battles that I faced

I am a Veteran of a Foreign War
where my country asked me to fight
And I often remember the ones who I fought for
and the ones I left behind.

Dedicated to those who fought and in memory of those who died.

Written for Jimmy by Josey McCall
I see the truth in your eyes and accept this truth has forever changed the perception of our lives.

Chapter Fourteen
Return to Work at Highlands Hospital

In 1979 the state began to phase out the TB Sanitarium and to fill the empty units with severe Mental Retardation and Developmentally Disabled patients. I worked for a few months in the role of a technician on one of the units that were established. LPN's were not used in that part of the facility, but they could work as technicians and they received the same pay as an LPN. During the few months I was in this role, I decided this was not a particular position I wanted to fill for an extended period of time. I decided to go back to school, get my Associate Degree in Nursing, and become a registered nurse.

I returned to Highland Hospital as an LPN staff nurse and applied for admission to the Associate Degree of Nursing program at Asheville Buncombe Technical Institute. Being back at Highlands would help to facilitate my attending this school and I would be closer to my children when I was working. I was accepted for the classes, starting in the fall of 1980. Meanwhile, I got reacquainted with old friends whom I had previously worked with at Highlands and made some new ones as well.

A few months after returning to the hospital, a young man named Randy, with whom I worked, invited me out. He was 7 years my junior but it did not seem to bother either of us. I accepted and I found I enjoyed his company. One evening, after going out for dinner, he invited me back to his house. I was still in a mind frame where I gauged the health of a relationship on its physical attributes and was not hesitant to become involved with Randy at what I saw as a non-threatening level. I later wrote the following poem about that particular evening and my associated thoughts.

Etched in Black

The night, pitch black, had settled on the eaves.
We made our way up steps we could not see.
You guided me.
The house was a mixture of vibrant, rustic
smells, and candle shadowed visions on the wall.
Music faded in and out,
just enough to know, that on some level it was there.
We chose to breathe, deeply, quietly,
Letting all things slip away, as then and there
Time and present were no bars around us.
I opened my eyes to blue deep pools above me
And a warm, moist tongue barely tracing the outline of my lips.
It traced further, to
My nose, my face, my earlobes, before

It returned to my lips again to gently,
searchingly enter.
Embers glowed, no words
Broke the silence as feelings set in motion
Began to seek their own way out.
A thousand times you brought
Me to the edge of recognition, then held
My gaze and allowed a moment's lapse.
The memory is etched like
Burnt wood upon the canvas of my mind.

This relationship lasted, off and on, about 2 years. Randy went to California during 6 months of that time and when he returned from out west we again began to spend time with each other. Often during the latter part of our relationship I would find I was trying to explain myself to Randy. I would apologize for a variety of situations and defend my perspective on issues, when there really wasn't a need. Then I felt frustrated because I wasn't sure exactly what I was trying to accomplish with this practice. There were so many things I did not understand and I apparently still had a lot of pain and uncertainty ahead of me to the point that I sometimes wondered if I would ever learn life's lessons in whatever manner it was supposed to occur.

Chapter Fifteen
In the Associate Degree Nursing Program

The 1980's were a busy and challenging time for me. I was accepted into the Associate Degree in Nursing program and started in the fall of 1980. I often worked weekends at the hospital, had school regularly Monday through Friday, and tried to take care of the children in between. My stress level was high much of those 2 years and my sons were frequently testing limits, in school and at home. They would sometimes be truant from school and I would receive calls at work telling me of their absence, and I would have to go home and physically take them to school. There were also times when they would have a rebellious attitude when we were all at home together. I did not associate my behaviors over the years as having any potential effect on how my sons were now behaving nor did I understand some typical childhood testing of normal limits and vies for my attentions away from my nursing studies.

During one of the rotations through the clinical area at a local hospital I was approached by my clinical instructor. She sat me down for a conference and indicated she was concerned that I was not coming to the clinical area prepared. It was midway through the rotation and she stated if I did not pull my grade up, I was going to fail this clinical period. I felt panicky in response, as I did not feel I could afford to fail. I needed to get back out into the work setting in full time employment as soon as possible. I had the monetary responsibility of the children and had many bills to pay. I felt I wouldn't have time to come back into the program if I did not pass it the first go around.

I did some hard looking in the mirror that night and realized I needed to make some serious changes in how I prepared for clinical. The next day, I made an appointment with a counselor friend who had previously worked at Highlands, to do what would now be called a crisis intervention. After the first appointment I shifted my workloads at home, I started getting a little more sleep, and I made being prepared for clinical a main priority.

Within the 3 week time period, I was able to pull the grade up enough to pass. I cannot remember the name of the instructor who supervised me for that rotation. I will always remember and appreciate the lessons she taught me about prioritization when taking care of myself and when providing nursing care to clients. The situation had also made me re-evaluate and reaffirm my commitment to finish the ADN program and to become a Registered Nurse. This had been my first time of seeking counseling on my own behalf. The benefits gained from this brief therapy would help to lay the foundation and acceptance of counseling as a viable support for me when I experienced another need for that support within the next few years.

During my pediatric rotation, I was assigned to the care of a child on the pediatric critical care unit of Mission Hospital. She had been placed in scalding hot water, by a parent, which resulted in extensive burns to her buttocks, legs, feet, and resulted in the webbing of her toes. The pediatrician in charge considered doing skin grafts to help these wounds heal more quickly. The child was unresponsive to attentions and treatment for a time and healing at first was very slow. With the constant and dedicated care of the physicians, nurses, and aides on the pediatric floor on which she was placed she did begin to improve. Once on the road to recovery, she healed at an amazing rate. No surgery was required. When she was discharged from the hospital, she was placed in the foster care of one of the attending nurses. Her future was more optimistic than it had been at the time of her admission.

When I first saw this child, I was horrified for her in consideration of the intense abuse that she had just experienced and for myself, for the flood of memories that washed over me. Her abuse brought out issues from my childhood that I had buried.

Ones I wanted to ignore and forget. In order to offer her compassionate, but effective care, I realized I first had to face than come to terms with portions of my own abused past. The following poem was the result of that night's efforts to deal with my own pain.

My role in this child's care was brief, but her life touched mine and changed it in a positive way. It has been many years, but I still remember seeing her at discharge, skip down the hospital hall with a bright smile on her face. She taught me that there is always hope for healing and I have often shared that message of recovery with others I have met along the way. In some ways, it shaped many of the future choices that I made, both in my personal life and work environment.

Catharsis

(Originally published in 2004 "The HeArt of Nursing" out of STTI's Press and republished in the second edition in 2006. Published here by prearrangement with HeArt of Nursing editor)

When I was a tender age, subjected to a father's rage,
Sure it was something I had done, a girl instead of son.
Anger boiled within my veins, then guilt for feeling—such a shame.
Father's one you do not question. What he does is law, no flexion.
But then I think and remember Mother.
I cried some tears, as did my brothers.
Pulled her out across the floor, slapped her face, her robe he tore.

Baby sister in her arms—he didn't care who he harmed.
So many years within my past, perhaps I had found my peace at last.
Until a child too young to fight, subjected too, without a flight,
Recalls the fears that once I held, and pulled out feelings I once felt,
Knocks so gently on the door behind which strong emotions store
And bids me deal with this again and realize what a war it's been
To fight my way and have a life and grasp this was an unearned strife
These things I see I buried deep, intending them to always sleep
But looking in a girl's deep blue eyes, I could not calm her tiny cries.
Until I faced what I went through and came to grips with my own truths,
Then with compassion I did share and give her total love—I cared.

I finished the ADN program and passed my state boards. Randy whom I was still dating spent the day with me prior to that night's graduation, in June of 1982. He brought a gift to the graduation ceremony of a dove necklace that I had been admiring that morning when we were browsing in the shops of Biltmore. I kept that gift for many years, until it eventually broke apart from age and use.

I noticed within the next few months after graduation that Randy seemed to be spending less and less time with me. He indicated that he was "very busy" and did not have time to spend with me. I found myself mooning over his lack of attention. In spite of the success I had just achieved by becoming an Associate Degree and then Registered Nurse I still tended to write a lot of melancholy poems related to being unhappy. I attempted to do some self-assessments with my writing and even though I could list positives about my skills and abilities I still could not seem to get past feeling sorry for myself. I thought I needed to have a male's complete and undivided attention all the time to be a complete person. I recognized I was at times afraid of or uncomfortable with, being alone. Randy had not given me any direct indication he wanted to end the relationship, but it was apparent to me at some level, even then, that we probably did not have much of a future together.

On an occasion in the fall of 1982, after an evening's brief visit together, I had smelled the scent of another woman on his face as I kissed him goodbye. I confronted him on this and he denied it with only minimal effort. I was irritated and frustrated, but rather than follow through with the confrontation, I just dropped it at that juncture. I continued to write about my insecurity and need for him throughout that fall while we were still occasionally seeing each other.

I recently found a journal with some writings from 1982,

where I had penned the following passage on one of the pages. It surprised me to realize the frame of mind I had been in at that time. I had not remembered having, or writing, on thoughts about suicide but apparently I had done so with intensity. Considering how enmeshed I was with Randy, I am not shocked.

"It's not usually just one thing that pushes a person to consider suicide, although it can be that last item on the stack that sparks the flame. It's trying and trying to accomplish something and then feeling like it is never enough. You are never good enough, you can rise above your station in life only so far then people tell you that you are not intellectual enough to make a difference. You try so hard, to fight what you were considered as a child; no good, woods brat, a bastard. I cannot stand the pain I stood while I was doing without money, heating with wood, raising two children alone, the long nights of studies, late hours, and working in between. I stood it all for two years, but I can't stand this and I'm just not sure how to change it. Then there is mother always "close to death". Sometimes I think if it weren't for the children, I might reach closer to that edge myself. We each, at times must live in our own man-made Hell. What is the magic answer, the key to pull us out? Find something to do, look at something more positive, use distractions of some kind and push yourself."

That's what I did, until I finally saw some light at the end of the tunnel over the next few years. Things continued to be sporadic between Randy and I for a few more months. In January 1983, he was invited to come to a small birthday party being held for me at a local pub. He came to the party in the company of a young lady. Shortly after they arrived I noticed that she sat on his lap and began kissing him on his face. Randy seemed to encourage her in this behavior. Either he had not been willing to tell me he wanted to break off, or he was afraid I would not hear what he was trying to say. Either way, the message that particular night, was clear enough.

Normally a light drinker, my response to the situation was far from healthy. I began to increase the amount and frequency of the alcohol I was drinking. I did not know it at the time, but some of my friends who were there at the party noticed this increase in my drinking. They had intervened by telling the waitress to make at least every other drink I ordered a straight cola. Jan and Randy had made a wise move on my behalf and I later appreciated that concern. I left the pub still very angry and generally intoxicated.

I can say now that I was subconsciously suicidal as I drove across a local bridge doing 90 miles an hour. I am sure the intensity was, in part, due to my general state of mind and part was due to the amount of alcohol I had consumed. I later had a more personal understanding, when there were clinical discussions, about the dangerous and negative impulses that can result from alcohol or other substance use and abuse. I was fortunate that night. There was no one else on the bridge and I made it home without being involved, or involving someone else in a wreck.

My ego was bruised and when I arrived home, I called Randy to cry out my ire. I left the impression I might do away with myself. I then left the phone off the hook and went to bed. The next day I promptly found someone else to date that worked with us and that Randy knew well. I could acknowledge, in this case, this was not going to be a permanent bond and I wanted to prove to myself and Randy how easily he could be replaced. I was bitter, petty, wounded and wanted revenge.

Thomas was a wild, motor cycle riding hippie and sweet as the taste of honey on a summer's day. He was a balm to my injured pride and we dated for a number of months. At one point in the relationship, he just stopped calling and coming by to see me. I accepted this change without question or pain and did not pursue an explanation from him for his disengaging from me and from the relationship. I was simply glad he had been there to help me through this rough time. I wrote an Ode to this kind and gentle giant of a man and he was pleased when I gave him a copy to read.

Ode to the Rider (Tom)

Shining knight
In black leather armor
Atop your jet black, two wheeled steed
Wind to your face
Sun to your back
Tattered scarf
Flung to the side
Long hair feathered back ,flowing loose in the breeze
Where will your travels take you
Over rivers
And to mountain tops
Through city streets
And hidden back roads
Are you searching for
Your own future`
Lifestyle
Truth
You pause a moment
And gently reach a hand
To those in need
Then you are on your way again
You catch the sunset's blaze
Across your eyes
With long slender fingers
You grip the handlebar
Chance guides your way and
Contentment is your goal
And may you find it
In your own grace and time

In life unhealthy habits sometimes change slowly.

Strangers

**Darkness parts
And light begins
As around us
The world does spin
I look in your eyes
You look in mine
And to all other things
For the moment we are blind
Warmth to the touch
Fragrance to the smell
Where things may lead
Only time would tell
I've known you forever
Although we have just met
As you looked in my soul
And I had no regrets
Forehead to forehead
Understanding I found
And to this moment
We both were bound
Parted as strangers
Lovers in flight
Always to have you
If for only tonight**

I was slowly learning some unhealthy characteristics that I possessed. I knew I was looking in the wrong places and for the wrong traits in a male, to experience a positive outcome in short, or long term relationships. I had a very unrealistic view of what constituted a satisfying and positive union. I still had not addressed or recognized changes that needed to occur within me and the choices I made in those with whom I associated and chose to date.

One of my coworkers asked me one day, when I seemed out of sorts, what it was that I was really looking for in life. I gave the answer that frequently came to mind "a sense of peace that always seemed to have eluded me".

I often felt like I was just going around and around in circles and not really getting anywhere with many personal aspects and relationships in my life. I became a Registered Nurse and changed positions and the types of responsibility I fulfilled within the hospital system. I enjoyed the work I did. I was supportive, caring, and effective in my work with the clients we served. If I could have just learned to be happy in my personal life.

Josephine McCall

Truth

So long the mind does hold the grief of childhood
As ancient eyes reflect the pain of youth
It is a truth that rage and fear
When clutched tightly to ones chest
Does but bar the door to Peace and Happiness

Chapter Sixteen
An Opportunity for Healing

Quest

The restless urge that surges through my veins
Will not be stilled
As with my mind my thoughts
Cannot be willed
I turn to seek the cause of my unrest
And find there is no answer to my quest

In 1982, after finishing my ADN classes and passing state boards, I moved into an RN nursing position at Highlands. I was working on one of the adult units during 1983, when a client who also happened to be a nurse, was admitted to the hospital for the psychiatric treatment of depression. In hearing her story of the sexual abuse she had experienced as a child and the resulting symptom's she experienced, I again had to come face to face with issues from childhood.

The result of my encounter with her was to recognize that my own mental health issues would need to be addressed before I could hope to comprehend what might be needed to provide her with support, understanding, and a means for to start on her journey to healing. I realized I would need to seek out my own treatment and attempt to find my own answers in hopes to bring some peace and understanding to my soul.

Rage

So much rage
Left over after all these years
Ignited so easy
Words fall like kindling to a dormant fire
Nitro
And I am suddenly engulfed in a roaring inferno
Boundaries of safety vaporize
Rage
Climbing from the depths of my very soul in the space of seconds
Burning, uncontrolled, chaotic, unreasonable and raw
Anger looking for a target on which to be unleashed
The searing pain
Anything to make it stop
Rage
Loosed, free, dark, boiling and powerful
Black as night, mindless, ugly, fury
Once spent
It leaves exhaustion and shame
In its wake
Bitter memories abound

Soul-searching

A sadness overwhelms
My dormant soul
And bids me shed a tear
And try not hold
The dam that dwells within
And begs release
For in its coarse
There's chance I may find release

I must move on

I cross the bridge
and look beyond
There lies a scene
Compared to none
A chance I take
In going there
But linger here
I do not dare
I must move on

Around the time I started into therapy, I also joined a singles club and support group, which had been advertised in a local paper. I figured this might be a place where I could develop some friends within a group setting and experience some shared support, with no strings attached. It was a good choice. It gave me an opportunity to develop a different understanding of responsibility to myself and to others. Within 2 years of joining this group I was also offered an opportunity to be in a position of leadership within the club. This turned out to be an chance for me to develop my own self-esteem in a positive way and this allowed me to grow as a person. This position gave me a chance to support others in their own journeys as a single person as they were trying to learn about and cope with the existence of a life alone and without the benefit of having a life partner.

In the past, I had tended to gravitate toward males for friendship and felt that was the only way I experience a meaningful relationship. I now recognized that an important part of continuing to heal was to learn to trust females. I had an unrealistic fear that friendships with women could become or be seen as something overly familiar. I began to realize I had personal responsibilities in recognizing and setting clear boundaries, in the roles of a friendship. I did not have to be a victim, or be taken advantage of, in any situation. I did not have to feel so challenged by another woman. With time and effort, I was able to develop real friendships with women, where previously I had viewed many relationships with females as transient, competitive, and undependable. I developed more faith in the person I was becoming and wanted to become in the future. I began to practice making choices in the safety of the singles group. I realized that I would sometimes make mistakes, but did not have to feel negative about that possibility as mistakes were a part of learning and a normal part of the growth process.

One of the friendships that grew out of this experience was with a lady named Teaka Gregg. I had continued to write and shared some of my works with Teaka. One particular piece I had written, during therapy, about my past was very raw and searing. With Teaka's help and guidance, it later became an essay that had more potential to help me to focus and then process the pain I was going through in a more productive manner. With this essay I was able to look at my life experience in a more congruent manner. This would begin to replace my overwhelming view of life being like loose puzzle pieces scattered in a totally disjointed manner. This essay also became a work that might be of support to others and be used as a tool for education around the confused feelings left over from experiences of abuse.

Teaka was a key to helping me turn this raging vitriol into an essay of worth. For that, I offer a statement of gratitude. She helped to guide me through the process and in so doing helped to be a part of those healing steps. I will be ever grateful for her support. Though we may go through years without contact, either of us can pick up the phone and call the other, or drop a line in the mail, and it's as if we had talked only yesterday. The following, more polished essay, is the result of much of the work we accomplished together.

<u>"One Nurse's View: The Hope Beyond Sexual Abuse"</u>

Being a nurse in a counseling role, it was particularly difficult for me to become the client but I was forced to do so. I needed to heal. The sexual, physical and emotional abuse of my childhood was long past, but it continued to traumatically affect my life. I was the victim still. I had no idea the abuse I experienced between the ages of 8 and 12 had influenced so many of my choices in life and was generally responsible for the emotional failures that usually followed.

I experienced many periods of remorse, depression, and dramatic despair—with "dramatic" being the key word. I sensed little fairness in life, always feeling I had to carry the heavier load. Through visibly public actions, I would seek the approval and admiration of others (needless to say I created animosity among a number of my co-workers along the way). I had no faith in my own judgment and would often look to others to validate the appropriateness of decisions that I made. I would mirror what I saw as a means of gauging what I was supposed to feel or do in emotional situations. If I made reference to my abuse, it was usually in a non-feeling, detached manner, vaguely alluded to as "my personal suffering" or "what I went through as a child."

I made many unwise choices and was often willing to take on more than I could handle. Then I became distraught and frustrated that I might let someone else or myself down. Over time, I realized I was angry with others for using me—and angry with myself for permitting it, but I felt unable to bring about a change. I was oversensitive to criticism and terrified of making mistakes (each one another bad mark on an already full blackboard). I found personal relationships with others lacking. Other people were never able to meet my needs and expectations. I did not consciously realize I sought to be dependent on others, nor could or did I see that the strengths I looked for in others were ones that I myself possessed. If I found myself in a situation where a broadly negative statement was made, I would personalize it, own it, it was mine.

Nightmares were common. They included scenes of exploding trains, airplane crashes, bursting dams, and role reversals— waking me to my own screams in the middle of the night. These dreams intensified when I was under increased stress and were one of a number of symptoms that finally forced me to seek help. I had many obsessive-compulsive tendencies, some beneficial and some not. I focused on other people's faults and mistakes to turn attention away from myself. In the end, instead, I drew negative attention for that practice.

If I was terrified of failure, I was also frightened of success, living as a person driven trying to prove with each mountain I climbed that I might be worthy. I often focused on the whole picture and tried to deal with everything all at once. I would sometimes become overwhelmed and anxiety ridden, almost paralyzed. This too was a symptom forcing me to seek help.

The last big indicator of my need for counseling was an over-identification with the clients under my care. I questioned how I could be effectively supportive to others when I myself was experiencing such a need. Although I did not know it at the time I began in treatment, many of the symptoms I was experiencing are common to Adults Molested As Children (AMAC's).

Counseling started for me when I experienced a drastic increase in the number of nightmares I was experiencing and I felt depression to the point that I had difficulty functioning in the work setting. I had trouble recognizing and maintaining healthy boundaries with clients who had similar histories to my own. I sought a social worker friend's advice on what approach I should take to deal with feeling so overwhelmed with all of these issues. Aware that I had been molested as a child she referred me to an upcoming workshop for AMAC's to be held the following month. Prior to the workshop I still did not recognize there could be any connections between the current problems I was experiencing and the sexual abuse of my childhood.

In the workshop, some of the initial barriers I had built around me over the years started to break down, as did the idea that the abuse could not be affecting my life now. It was frightening and disquieting to realize how many others suffered the same kind of feelings that I did. This sharing with others in the group began to take away from some of the uniqueness that my secret abused past had carried. I started with individual therapy sessions in the following week. I then joined a regular AMAC support group formed as a result of the workshop.

The process was slow and painful, and one of the first and biggest steps I had to take was to realize it wasn't my fault. It took hearing this statement over and over and over again before I finally began to believe it. For years I felt I had allowed, even somehow had asked for, this abuse to happen. At last I realized that as a child, I had been powerless to control the situation, but that as an adult, I could redirect my life, make valid choices, and create healthier options for myself.

I was impatient, wanting everything to change at once, looking for "greater leaps" rather than "smaller steps." I recognized during therapy that many of my personal and professional relationships were like replays from my childhood. I was frequently competitive, peevish, and immature, especially in response to confrontation.

I found I was afraid to give up my anger in life, feeling it was the fuel I had lived on, uncertain with what it could be replaced. I discovered with surprise and relief that I was actually committed to life.

After much work, I was able to put aside a lot of the guilt I had carried for years. I realized I was not responsible for everyone else's feelings, welfare, and choices—especially not those of my parents or other family members. I was responsible only for my own feelings and actions. I began to explore and expand and to find more solid ground. I finally realized my life was not going to totally change, nor would I be able to completely eliminate certain learned behaviors. I could and did learn to mediate my behaviors to a point where they were more appropriate and acceptable. I also became more realistic in my expectations of myself and others. With practice I learned how to replace old unhealthy practices with ones that were healthier and more productive

As my rigidity diminished, my flexibility improved. I grew more able to accept criticism and see my problems more objectively. I found I could trust and share with group members and could deal with problems I had never been able to face before in my life. I learned how to be successful.

Group and individual process varies in duration. My individual treatment lasted a year and a half. My involvement in the group therapy over time changed and after a time it became a client run support group which was alternately held in individual client's homes. I stayed in that group for another 6 months. It was validating when it reached the point where I was strong and independent enough to recognize it was time to withdraw from the group.

At one time, prior to treatment I visualized my life as a vase, shattered and glued back together many times, always with fragments missing and always dark and empty. At the end of counseling, I saw not a vase but a person, solid and whole, with both strengths and weaknesses like any other individual in the world. I found I was free to learn from my mistakes and finally willing to give myself that chance. I actually began to heal.

Clarity

Half forgotten dreams tumble softly to the ground
And altered hopes of times gone by are mine
Where once I pleaded for your love
Now I no longer have the need
The perception of my world
Is auburn haze, soft and warm
And now when it is time
I can in my aloneness find Peace

An Open Letter to the child of Abuse written with a hope to help others

I cannot take away the monsters that lurk beside your bed, in the corners of your home, or are sometimes hidden in the shadows of houses proclaimed for worship.

I cannot bar the windows for your protection or stop the fearful storms that rage within your soul I cannot tell you that life is fair and safe because you already know it is a promise that cannot always be kept, even in the best of circumstances.

I cannot stop the fear you feel when you are threatened with harm to yourself or others you love should you speak of the abuse nor can I prevent the statements abusers lash out that "should you tell you will not be believed."

I cannot tell you unjust deeds will always be punished in equal amounts to the crimes that are committed or the agony that you suffer, even though that justice should be the case.

I cannot tell you life will ever be easy for those who are violated and have experienced abuse at the hands of someone who has been named trustworthy.
I cannot resolve all the doubts and fears that often go around and around in your mind or deny for you that the abuse occurs.

What I can tell you is that physical wounds will heal and given the chance you can in time and with effort find your own truths. That the abuse you experience as a child is not your fault and is fully the responsibility of the adult who has misused you.

They have taken advantage of their being older and having power over you as a child. That you can come to realize love is not found by abusing yourself through the use of drugs, by seeking out those who would continue to misuse you, or by molesting someone else who is younger and weaker then yourself-this abuse of others will not help to ease the pain and sense of loss you may feel and can reinforce the guilt that you may already experience.

Please know that it is a path many who have been victims have followed but for your own sake and the sake of other children it needs to be avoided and if it now occurs it needs to stop.

I can tell you the secret of abuse can continue to hold power over you as long as you keep it clutched tightly and protectively against your chest. When shared in a support group setting the abuse loses some of the horror and shame such a secret can carry.

I can tell you that you are not alone, that many others have faced and are facing fears and anguish such as you are going through. Although it has taken them a long time, many have gotten beyond just survival, and now live a fuller more peaceful life.

I can tell you there is help and hope beyond the abuse but you must hold on and believe in yourself until the time arrives when you are set free from this bondage you did not ask for.

I don't always know where you are or what pretense you must go through for the sake of your sanity or for your immediate physical safety but I do know you are there and in need.

During, and after completing that therapy, I continued to work at Highland Hospital, in the role of an RN staff nurse. An opportunity came up for me to take a full charge and management position on one of the units. I said no. I was realizing that it was better for me to wait until I was ready for some advances in responsibility, rather than jump in head first. I recognized a lot of the politics and rivalry's that existed in that offered position and I decided to avoid being in that particular conflicted role. If I moved into a management position it would be in my own time and at my own choice.

With my having a secure job, a good income, and a little better sense of myself I now turned with determination toward trying to be a better mother. I wanted to work on relationship issues with my sons. I was having increased problems in dealing with both of them, but I was having the most difficulties with my oldest son. With the experience of my own counseling I had developed an awareness and understanding that there were areas of my children's life with which I had dealt in an unhealthy manner. I was beginning to be more open to learning what we, as a family, could do differently. I could not go back and undo what was already done. Where previously I had difficulty setting some limits, I now came to understand if something didn't feel right, then I needed to say no to both of my son's request.

Some unrealistic yearnings and expectations take time to fade and change. I still missed not having a steady mate, but I was able to realize this yearning was more of a habit and was a result of my tendency to become dependent on someone in response to life's stresses. With increased awareness I was more able to pull back and let life just happen for a while. I had also decided it was better for William and John, if I just put dating on the shelf and concentrated more on us as a family. The major exception I made to this decision was when I ran into Lee, whom I hadn't seen in years. I dated him for about three weeks and very quickly recognized this would be a brief association. I did, however, decide to stay in it long enough to see what I could learn from the experience. Three weeks was long enough to recognize that I had made a number of changes in the way I interacted with men and Lee in particular. I found I was looking for something healthier in relationships. I realized he was not able to connect on a more mature and healthier level then we had shared in the past. I felt okay with ending this relationship and was able to move on.

Chapter Seventeen
Personal Growth and Exploration

I continued as a member of the singles group and found it was a satisfying and gratifying activity in which to be involved. I was asked to run for president of the group in 1984. I agreed to do so and was elected. We grew from 80 to 200 members during that year. In 1987, I would again be asked to run and serve an additional term. That second term would be the last time I would be available to fill that position.

My first term was an exciting time for me. On a whim, I had, on my own, attended a workshop entitled "Pathways to Progress" held at the Asheville Civic Center. The experience of the workshop gave me the idea for our singles group to put on a workshop for singles. I made the suggestion at one of our regular meetings and the response to the idea was very positive. Those most interested in participating were organized into a committee to explore the feasibility of developing a workshop. After much discussion, we gave the anticipated workshop a title "Fulfilling the Promise of Every Single Day".

I sought out the director of the hospital where I worked, to see if we would be able to procure Homewood School (located on the hospital grounds) as a possible site for the workshop. I was encouraged to meet with Dr. Darwin Dorr, the head of the psychology department of the hospital and the chair of the "Highland Hospital Foundation". The willingness of the hospital and Dr. Dorr to be involved in the event and the hospital boards confirmation that it could be held on hospital grounds, helped to validate the authenticity of our efforts. I learned some of the many steps that would be required in order to go forward with our plans.

Without Dr. Dorr's guidance, we would never have been able to achieve such a successful endeavor. He, his wife, and I have maintained a correspondence over the years that started with that first meeting about the workshop. They are both supportive of mental health education and treatment and are a treasure to those with whom they are associated. He was at the time of the writing of this book head of the Psychology Department of Wichita University and his wife Stephanie fulfilled a position working with a special needs population.

The work to create this workshop was exhilarating and exhausting. I learned this was a project that required many hands and long hours. Those were given freely by the board members of the singles group and many of the singles club members.

Individuals, like Evie Bryant and Sarah McGinnis were instrumental in helping this conference to happen. A number of the staff that worked at the hospital participated and were willing to help us see this workshop succeed.

I felt the workshop was as successful as it could have possibly been. It was not a nursing endeavor, but I found that my nursing experience certainly helped to make it happen. The experience of being in the singles group and helping with this workshop made me a better person and thereby a better nurse. An appreciation gift to the Highland Foundation for the support provided to the singles club and the singles workshop was presented to Dr. Dorr at a dinner provided in his honor. I think that participating in this workshop and all that was entailed in making it happen was one of the high points of my career and my life. The experience served me and I think all of those who were involved well.

In early fall of 1987, we received a large increase in pay at the hospital and I decided it was time to make my first purchase of land and a home. The situation with my oldest son had continued to be difficult and had reached a point of need for major change. I told him of my decision to invest in a home. I offered him the choice that he could move with us and work on some of those needed changes or he could stay in the house we rented and up until he graduated I would provide some monetary support and assistance. He was due to graduate within the next 6 months and I indicated I would help him pay his monthly expenses if he chose to stay in the home and while he finished school. There was wood to use in the stove when it was needed for heat and William was very familiar with managing the wood stove. There were groceries and a large supply of can goods he would have available to eat and he now had a regular income, as he was working part time at a local seafood restaurant. William could also take some of his meals at the restaurant where he was employed. He indicated he preferred to stay in the home. John and I would be moving into a home that I would purchase. This came to be the pivotal point of change and separation for us as a family.

Chapter Eighteen
A Change in Life's Direction

Mountain Cultures and Memories

Cold winter nights spent by crackling fires, sometimes built just
for warmth and sometimes to keep the thump keg roaring,
Long, rough and muddy roads climbed by horseback, wagon, or on
two feet, hopefully with boots on for protection from the stones.
Maybe, on rare occasion, slow trips taken by model A's or T's up
steep cliffs leading to places high in the mountains, that are
surrounded by woods filled with deer and bear, tracks and scat.

Loud screams echo off the rock walls from occasional panthers
and cries like a child often emitted from a bobcat calling her kits.
Screeches sound from hawks as they fly down on their next meal,
whippoorwills' calls heard at dusk
a rain doves cries foretell a change in the coming weather
deep-throated frogs call for their mates, cicadas' and crickets sing
just as dusk starts to fall
grey squirrels, boomers, and flying squirrels chatter to each other
in warning at the carnivores prowling on the ground and gliding in
the sky
water gurgles down and across the crest of a ridge, racing faster as
it moves toward the waterfall then on to merge with a splash in the
river of a valley far below

Snow storms were measured in feet not inches and wind blew that
would often bring large solid looking timber to the ground
the sound of gunshots in the middle of the night paired with the

yelps and barks of baying hounds and a noted and prominent
absence of the howls of timber wolves.
Land tilled with the hand and plow, seeds and plants scattered on
the rocky ground of a hillside, some may grow, some may not
water drawn from a spring and carried to the house in buckets,
children born at home with an old midwife to give assistance,
some lived some died,
birth, death and marriage notations made in a family bible and
maybe taken to a county seat if and when time allowed for the trip.

Rattlesnakes and copper heads lay coiled under rocks or inside the
pile of firewood lain by the door death sometimes unexpected
from these hidden vipers
hands roughened by outside work, the building of a home,
exposure to the weather, and laundry done on a washboard,
chickens clucking and pecking at insects on the ground and pulling
grass around their straw filled nest full of eggs set to soon hatch.
Hunters and farmers as young as 8 years old sometimes with miles
of distance to walk to get to a small one room school house before
time for farm work and hunting could be done
Old time gospel music heard over crackling radios or radiating on
Sunday from the church centered a number of miles from home
Ginseng, lady slippers, ramps, blood root, plant life of beauty and
some used for medical needs
May-apples, branch mustard, and branch lettuce, growing wild and
untamed.
Herbs used for ills, food and as spices for the table.

Majestic hemlocks with broad lacy limbs big enough to create a
shield from rain and snow now slowly dying from infestations
Blueberries, buck berries, and service berries picked from native
bush and tree to be eaten raw or canned on a cook stove against a
winters need

old coins hidden in jars under the porch and musty dollar bills stuffed in gunny sacks, buried somewhere in an out of the way place and maybe never found or maybe rotted with age
Unexplained noises in the middle of the night and tales of those who's death has not stopped the movement of their wandering souls
Always a rifle by the door against dangers from day, night, and unknown strangers roaming in the hills
A past history and life that may not be so distant to children born in the back hills of Buncombe, Haywood, Jackson, Macon and Madison County over the last 50 years.
Home places and locations with names like Pin Hook Valley, Punching Cap Gap, Graveyard Fields, and the Devils Court House Rock.
Towns like Sunburst built to support railroads used for logging, now buried under water and all but forgotten.
Some of the old ways, memories and determination to survive still live on in generations of families who still call these mountains home.
And are a part of the fiber from which Pauline's life was woven and from which she gained the strength and tenacity to survive the struggles she faced throughout her life.

New Beginnings

Music
Pure
Sincere
Throbs deep within my soul
And I would have you share it
By candle light or dark
It is a start

Josephine McCall

Kenneth McCall

December 2nd 1987, was a cold and blustery day. John and I had moved into a 2 bedroom trailer that I was buying on time along with the property on which I had it been set up. John was visiting his brother. I was off for the weekend and slept late then decided to make a trip to the flea market. I, dressed in old baggy pants, a loose pullover sweater, a floppy coat and my oldest but most comfortable pair of boots. I knew I was not shopping for anything more than a pre-Christmas day out for fun. I was this day comfortable in my old clothes and my own skin.

I got to the market late morning and as it was just before Christmas, all the vending spots were filled. I noticed a group of cut Christmas trees along the fence and overheard a buyer asking the vendor how much they would cost. He answered, $10.00 each. I was not planning to buy a tree, but I was curious how this man could sell these trees so cheap, when all the other trees I had seen were being sold for $30 to $50 each. I asked him if he would like a cup of coffee when I came back that way, as I was interested in talking to him about the trees. With a half grin on his face he replied yes. When I returned, I had his coffee in one hand and hot chocolate for me in the other.

We talked about Christmas trees in general and he told me

that he was in the shrubbery and plant nursery business. He had this batch of trees left over after making a larger sale and thought they might go well at this flea market. When I asked him about the prices, he smiled and said "there are a lot of women trying to raise children who may have a hard time affording the cost of a tree. At this price they were more likely to be able to afford one. Besides if they don't have the money, I might just give them one anyway." I felt a small catch in my chest and I thought "how sweet".

He was dressed in sturdy overhauls, had a brown beard, brown hair that reached and covered his ears, and eyes as blue as the sky. Kenneth said he had a phone number from one county, an electric service from another and his address was in a third county. I was intrigued. We talked for probably about an hour on a variety of topics. The temperature was steadily dropping and it was getting very cold. I said goodbye and he gave me a business card that had his phone number on it. He told me to call him sometime and "maybe we could go out". Just before I left, he handed me a Christmas tree. It was small enough for me to carry easily and large enough to fit snugly in a corner of the front room of the trailer. I hadn't planned on having a tree, but now I would be setting one up.

I happened to be off again the next day and couldn't resist

the urge to go back to the flea market. Kenneth was there, but in a different location. We again talked for a while and he introduced me to his father, who had also been there the day before but had stayed generally in the background. His father was smiling and a jovial man. I did not stay as long this time and when I started to leave, he handed me the makings for a wreath. I sensed this was a different kind of man that I had met and I was awed and surprised by those indefinable differences.

I called the number on the business card the next week, as the singles club was having a Christmas dance and I wondered if he would be interested in going. An older female answered the phone, which put me off a little bit and when I asked if Kenneth was home, I was told he was out of town, delivering trees. I decided to drop him a line to his address and figured I would not hear from him again.

Kenneth knocked on my door, early one morning, a few days later while I was still resting in bed. He was decked out in a cowboy shirt, blue jeans, boots and a cowboy hat. We talked for a time and planned our first date. He offered to take me to a place in Tennessee for our first dinner out or basically anywhere I wanted to go which had somewhat surprised me that he would offer to go that far. After a few months courtship we moved in together. We then married on June 25th 1989. I wrote the following invitation and sent it out to our friends and family. It is a reflection of the area and culture in which we lived.

An Appalachian Mountain Wedding Invitation

From the Mouth of the Valley rolls the morning mist
the sun has yet to filter through the clouds
the mountains range wide with blue cloaked arms around
their charge
The earth is hushed, suspended by a breath on a dew bound web
The day awakes and the journey begins for two people who
will this day become as one
as they stand in Gods chapel at the top of the world
You are invited to join them at the end of their journey alone
and the beginning of their life together,
already pledged to each other they will now speak their
vows before God and man
As cardinals pair and mate for life so will they trove to
each other as man and wife

Chapter Nineteen
Unchartered Waters and Family Relationship's

Our first years together were full of major rises and falls. I had matured a good bit and knew what I didn't want in a marriage. I was, however, still unsure what elements needed to be included for us to have a healthy relationship and a good marriage and life together. Kenneth's first wife had died nine months before we met. He had gone looking for someone to help fill the emptiness of her loss and he had not allowed himself time to grieve her passing. I recognized this unresolved grief in him and tried to allow him the time and space he needed for that process to occur.

Kenneth's family was close knit and His parents lived right next door to our trailer. I was not used to being in this close a proximity to in-laws and it was something to which I had to adjust. Kenneth was constantly in his parents company and at their home, and there were times I felt somewhat like an extra wheel. It took me years to come to terms with that difference in culture and with the isolation of being at least 45 minutes from the nearest town.

At times, we were cut off from the rest of the world, especially when the snow would make travel out of the valley almost impossible. There were also times when I felt like I had to sit on my hands to hold still long enough to give this new life a chance to work and to get use to this very different kind of lifestyle.

My youngest son moved with us to our home in Jackson County. He at first seemed okay with this move and different life, but then, within weeks he again began to stay out of school, which was a habit he had developed prior to our coming to Pin Hook. He would claim illness or just oversleep and miss the bus. I left for work before the school bus ran so was not there to prompt or supervise him. He seemed to ignore my statements and concerns about his constant absences and he was resistant to Kenneth's encouragement for him to attend school.

An incident occurred where John was angry and he attempted to involve Kenneth in a physical fight to prove some kind of point. Kenneth did well, by simply allowing John to swing at him without actually letting him make physical contact with his own body. John exhausted himself without having actually hit anyone. At one point, prior to mine and Kenneth's wedding, I had attempted to get John some counseling, but he did not respond well to the attempt and the psychologist who tested him said John really did not exhibit symptoms of depression. I did not catch the hint that John could have more intense issues hiding underneath his external presentation. I did note the therapist seemed glad that I had someone of support who had come into my life so that I would not be dealing with John's behavior totally on my own. I could say I had wished he had warned me of the suspicions he might have held about Johns potential issues but I do not know if I would have listened if he had expressed them at the time.

A few months after we were married, Kenneth and I decided to take a trip out west. He indicated he wanted to take his dad with us on this vacation. I had mixed feelings about taking someone else along, as this was sort of our honeymoon, but I felt like it was something with which I could live. The trip lasted two weeks. It was a fast paced, energized vacation and we had a wonderful time. I had never been further west than Tennessee and taking this trip was a thrill for me. John stayed in our trailer and had meals with my mother-in-law while we were gone. He was supposed to attend school but again would often find ways to avoid going. In hindsight he manipulated my mother-in-law much in the same ways that he had manipulated me. I had just not realized how charming to a fault that John could be until many years later.

Kenneth's Dad seemed to be a lucky man while we were

on this trip. He would often find items that others had lost. When we went through Yellowstone Park, he found a man's watch, we went through a small town in South Dakota, and he found someone's Driver's License, then he later found a lady's precious stone ring in a parking lot. He later gave it to Pauline as a gift when we returned home from our trip. During this adventure, I realized Herbert had never been out west either. He was a kind hearted man and I grew to appreciate him a good deal, starting while we were on that trip. We listened to music on cassette tapes, Will the Circle be Unbroken, Volume 2 in particular, and would sing along with the music while we were traveling. We ate sandwiches for most meals and alternated sleeping in the front of the truck on its seats, with sleeping on a mattress we had in the bed of truck. We stopped anywhere it looked interesting and spent an occasional night at a motel. We went to Washington State and stayed with relatives of Kenneth's family, on a July 4th weekend. There were fireworks everywhere and the state of Washington was beautiful.

We made a stop, at a place called Bear Country USA, and I saw more bears in that one drive through than I would have seen at a dozen zoos. We saw mule deer in field's off to the side of the main road and huge elk in private pastures. We explored the site of Custer's last stand and viewed Mount Rushmore. We toured a snake display that was filled with live snakes and preserved dead ones realistic enough to frighten when they were observed in the tinted and dim light. Kenneth jumped, when I touched his shoulder as he was looking at a darkened display that was tucked away in an alcove of a small cave.

We saw the badlands of the Dakotas and viewed some of the prehistoric animal bones recovered from that area. We saw the glitter and felt the weight of Black Hills gold sold in small shops along the roadside. We visited old-timey museums set up beside the highways and small stores that held rustic jewelry. I also had my first, and only, stop and shop buffalo burger on this trip. I can still remember the leather like quality of the meat when I tried to chew it. I had been warned by Kenneth and Herbert it would be tough, but was determined to try it out anyway. I was glad I did not lose a tooth. We all returned from the trip in good health and good spirits.

In the fall of 1989, close to his 16th birthday, I had talked about sending John to Asheville to live and explored the possibility of his being an emancipated minor with the local legal authority. My in-laws encouraged me to wait and give him more of a chance to remain in Pin Hook. Around his birthday he had asked me if he could spend a couple of weeks with his brother in Asheville. William now had his own apartment and had seemed to have settled down. William was in agreement to the visit, so I took John to Asheville in high spirits at this prospect of a break from the mountain life and of spending time with his brother. After I had taken John to Asheville, my husband and in-laws indicated they did not want John to return to Pin Hook. He had destroyed property of which I was not made aware until after I had taken him to his brothers. It was ironic that I had discussed the option of letting him become an emancipated minor a few weeks before his visit to Asheville and they had encouraged me to wait. This would have allowed him to make and be responsible for his own life decisions in an established and legalized manner.

It was frustrating for me to then be presented with the statement the family did not want him to come back to the valley after I had so recently forgone that decision. When I gave him the news of this discussion, he reacted in a pleased manner, asking his brother if he could live with him for a time. William stated yes, and John officially moved back to Asheville and for a while became his own boss. He never returned to live in Pin Hook, although he was later able to come for brief visits. After John married he, his wife and children were for a time frequent visitors to our mountain.

Within two years of this trip out west, Herbert decided he wanted to get a travel camper, and then all four of us could make a trip out west. The trip took place prior to the diagnosis of a number of medical problems that my father-in-law had developed. We took that second trip in the company of Kenneth's mom and dad in a camper. The trip was great and we did a lot of site seeing and generally explored a lot of the country. We were gone from Pin Hook for three weeks. These were some of the best memories I carry to the present of us as a family together,

I had been in Jackson County for a little over two years, when a crisis arose within my own family, related to my mother and brother Eddies living situation. Their home was being condemned and they were going to be made homeless. My sister had done all she could to try and repair the old house, but it was an imposing and unrealistic task. Mother was a hoarder and it was a losing battle that Margie could not win.

My in-law's offered to let my mother rent a trailer from them and live in the valley with me, Kenneth, and the rest of his family. Mother had many cats, and my in-laws said they would (and they did) build her a lot the cats could live in. With quite a production, she, my brother and the cats were moved to Pin Hook.

Within a number of months, my Mother and brothers presence in the valley became an added stress to mine and Kenneth's marriage. I often felt pulled between my Mother and brother and my husband and his family. Mother's pattern of being a hoarder in the home in Asheville began to develop in the trailer in Pin Hook. I realized Eddie had some of the same kind of habits and practices that mother did. Eddie also had poor hygiene and did not like to bathe. These issues began to be more obvious shortly after they moved into the trailer in Pin Hook. Other additional negative dynamics that existed within Eddie's behaviors came to light over the next few years.

Kenneth's family had a small Christmas Tree farm and after I had resigned from my job at Highlands Hospital, I would help with the farming and potting that took place. I continued to write and even sent some of my work to a few nursing magazines. My works received commendations, but none were at that time considered for publication.

At Christmas we would set up a camper and sell Christmas Trees in various places locally and later Tennessee. The first couple of years, either Herbert or Pauline stayed with us during our time on a sales lot. Pauline would make a few Christmas Wreaths to sell and cooked most meals. As years went by it became just Kenneth and I who would stay for the length of the season, with occasional visits made from either Herbert or Pauline. This time together helped us to become closer and we worked together like the team we were. It felt less stressful, and family issues and problems faded to the background. This gave me more hope for our long range future.

I remember wintry days at the lot, when we would be so cold from the rain and snow it might take hours to get rid of the chill after we closed the lot down. Sometimes in the evening, when sales would stop, we would fix homemade spaghetti and warm up by the small heaters we kept going in the camper. It was more like a bohemian lifestyle and it suited us well. Those were some of my fondest memories and some of our happiest times together.

YULETIDE

Bells and bows
Long distance calls
Christmas trees alight

Children's eyes
And family ties
A time of Peace and quiet

Merry cheeks
And closet peeks
Reverence of the soul

Christmas shops
And sweet gum drops
A time to wish for snow

Nativity scenes
And reds and greens
A warmth within the heart

Turkey dinner
First of winter
Natures work of art

Candles lit
A time to sit
And wrappings on the floor

Christmas Nog
And Yule log
Wreaths upon the door

Gingerbread house
And sleeping mouse
A star atop the tree

Cedar pines
And holly vines
A child that set men free

Shopping Malls
And mistletoe
Greeting cards to send

Christmas here
A glad New Year
And fellowship of friends

Times changed and it became apparent that more money was being spent on the cultivation of the trees than was being made by their sales, so the family finally decided to stop raising and then selling Christmas Trees. I did not miss the cold and wet weather, but I did miss the closeness and time Kenneth and I had to share with each other on the Christmas tree sales lots.

Josephine McCall

Kenneth

When I think of you, I think of being rolled up in a warm blanket in front of a fire

I think of rain on a tin roof in the middle of the night
I think of an early morning sunrise on the Parkway and shadows cast by the moon
Late at night

I think of deer hidden in the woods and rabbits running through the garden
I think of hard work and sweat running down your face, some pain and going until

You were finished or dropped, whichever came first I think of everyday living and looking forward to the future and not back to the past

I think of sharing, protecting, and being protected
I think of fire and heat, then softness and Peace
I think of snow in the valley and the thousand of memories we already share

I think of our life together

I think of happiness
I think of love
I often think of you

In 1993, Kenneth's dad became ill, and with much encouragement from us all, he finally agreed to make an appointment and go see a doctor. Herbert had a long history of alcohol abuse and prior to his appointment, he had also exhibited symptoms of high blood pressure. This was the reason he finally agreed to go for the visit.

Results from some of the lab work drawn on Herbert identified an increase in his blood sugar and later results of his PSA test showed an elevation, which can be indicative of prostate cancer. He was able to stop drinking without evidencing any withdrawal symptoms, which was surprising to me considering the frequency of his use of alcohol.

After a consultation with a urologist and completion of a number of diagnostic procedures, he was found to have Prostate Cancer. He had radical prostate surgery and later radiation treatment. Throughout his lengthy treatment, he saw a total of seven different physicians. I did transition notes from one Dr.'s visit to the next and from one physician to another. This seemed beneficial in his treatment and helped to create a smoother transition in his care. It also gave me an opportunity to develop case management experience. After Herbert completed this major cancer treatment, he seemed to stabilize and gratefully, for a time, he was symptom free. We were all glad for what came to be a reprieve for he and the family.

Happy Brown was a crusty old salt, who we knew well from the flea market that we often visited. He had lost one of his legs while “resting” on a set of railroad tracks, when he had been a young man. He had apparently been intoxicated, and had fallen asleep on the tracks. During the time that Herbert was receiving treatment I was also experiencing increased stress from my family which effected my general attitude. Kenneth and I would occasionally stop by to see Happy, where he had a regular stall set up at the local farmers market. Sometimes we would chit chat and sometimes, he would buy any plants we had left over from selling a load at the flea market. He often swore like a sailor in conversations but, underneath all the rough talk, he evidenced a caring heart. When we would visit, he would always ask me how I was doing and likely as not, I would complain about one or another of the problems that we were facing in life.

On one particular day he responded, "Joey I'm going to quit asking you how things are, because when you answer it’s always bad and you never have anything good to say. If things are that bad, maybe you need to think about doing something about it”. It made me stop and think. I told him, you know, I think you could be right. After that visit, it made me consider if I was always focused on the negative, what could or should I do to change that attitude and or situation. I looked at life, what I felt like was the hardest issues for me to deal with, and what options I might develop to make things better for me. I had also acknowledged to myself that I was having continued periods of intense depression and perhaps that was a part of the problem.

In the same time frame and on a follow up visit with Herbert's regular physician, a PSA level was drawn on him. Herbert's PSA had again started to rise and after a diagnostic workup by his cancer specialist, it was found his cancer had spread to his bones. His cancer diagnosis was changed from the initial curable diagnosis to a terminal status. Any treatment he received thereafter, would be focused on decreasing his pain. I knew I would be helping some with his care throughout the rest of his illness and his life.

I then looked at a variety of possibilities for myself for the immediate future. I decided I needed to either go back to work, become certified in my field, or go back to school. It seemed like the best option for me, would be to go back to school. This way, I would have some flexibility in my schedule and I would still be able to help out with my father-in-laws care as his health declined.

My husband and I made a specific trip back to visit Happy and I told him how much I appreciated his caring enough to point out where my focus had been. I also told him that I would be going back to school and that I certainly did have some things to be happy about. He seemed pleased to have contributed to this change in life's focus for me. I had also had some nightmares about his health and encouraged him strongly to have a checkup. He indicated he would.

Even with the determination to make things better and to try to look at the world in a more optimistic manner, I still continued to experience mood swings. When I felt down, I simply tried to deal with the feelings and focus on the issues that required the most immediate attention. This would depend on what the greatest need was, at any particular time.

Chapter Twenty
Completion of Bachelor of Science in Nursing Education

I made an appointment at the Western Carolina University Nursing Admissions' office housed at the University of North Carolina at Asheville. When I went for my initial meeting regarding the Capstone program, my appointment was with a very familiar former acquaintance. At that time, Jeanne Howe was the head of the Capstone Program. I was surprised and pleased to see her. She explored with me what would be needed, in order for me to be accepted into the program. There were several courses I would need to take at the community college level and I would need transcripts from previous schools and programs I had attended. It was exciting to again be taking another step in my nursing career and learning new information.

I started at Southwestern Community College in the fall of 1996, and took Humanities, Math and English courses, to meet transfer requirements I would need for Westerns program. I enjoyed the classes and was able to work at a slower rate than in the previous years when I had gone to school and worked steady jobs at the same time. I found a lot of encouragement for my writing and began to write more in earnest. An instructor named Owen Gibby was one of my English teachers who evaluated and praised my work and encouraged me to continue to write. I remember feeling supported and inspired by his efforts to enlighten those of us in his classes.

I continued to experience conflicting feelings about being in my marriage to Kenneth and the writing helped me to gain a different perspective on those feelings. I often felt like I was on the proverbial fence and didn't know which way to go. I did know I had enough on my plate and did not want to make any other major changes in my life at the time. I also knew that my father-in-laws cancer, the stress of having two of my own family members living in the valley, and the clannishness of my in-laws and the rest of Kenneth's family were all contributing factors to what I was feeling.

I continued to put personal life and decisions on hold and really just focused on school, my father-in-laws medical needs, and simply living from one day to the next. Because of the ongoing depression and with the recommendation of a friend, I also started to take St. Johns Wart. It was an herb that was highly recommended to assist with the symptoms of depression. I did notice within the next few months, that I was feeling better and was somewhat less depressed.

I made new friends with other students at Southwestern Community College. Some of them were also preparing for the nursing program at WCU. It was interesting to find other students who were experiencing some of the same kind of stressors I was and it helped to hear what they had to say about school and about life. It was a busy year, but I graduated with honors from the community college, and was now ready to take that next step toward my Bachelor of Science in Nursing Degree.

I returned to WCU with my pre-entry requirements in hand. Dr. Howe and I explored the classes I would need to take in the Capstone Program and established when I would start into the nursing classes. I began in the fall of 1997. It was a different experience, taking classes at the university level, rather than at the community college.

I enjoyed the challenges of these new classes and it helped me to see nursing from a more academic perspective. This was where and how I first met professors such as Sharon Jacques, Vincent Hall, and Carol Stevens. I came to understand there were many reasons why nurses do what they do and in what way many of the nursing decisions, related to patient care, were made.

In hindsight, the several semesters seemed to go by

quickly, but during the time of the classes, it seemed like time passed very slow. I was fortunate enough to make good grades and to graduate with honors when all the classes were completed.

It was during one of my nursing classes that I was encouraged to join a professional nurses association and choose to join the American Nurses and North Carolina Nurses Association. I have continued to connect to that association to the present although over the last few years have not been as active as I was the first ten years.

I was still very involved with my father-in-laws and mother-in-laws care at home. Pauline had a total knee replacement within that year and several months before my father-in-laws death. His condition declined after her return home and as she recovered from her first surgery. He died within a week of my graduation from WCU. It was a bitter sweet time for me and a sad time for the whole family.

The fall after I graduated from WCU, I was invited to join Sigma Theta Tau International. I felt honored to have been asked and became a member a short time later. The next year STTI sent out a request for submissions of art and written work to be considered for display as a part of an exhibit called the HeArt of Nursing. I sent in a submission of the poem Catharsis and it was chosen, as one of 50 total selections, for display at the next conference from hundreds that were entered from inside and outside of the country. Our local Eta Psi Chapter, of which I was a member, provided me with an opportunity to attend that conference and be able to display this submission.

During the conference, I was encouraged to consider running for the office of the president of the Eta Psi Chapter of STTI. I had thoroughly enjoyed the conference and was energized by all the nurses who had been present. They exhibited a total commitment to providing excellent and professional nursing care. I did feel I had the skills and could, with support, fill the role of president of our chapter. With numerous encouragements, I ran for that office. I was elected to a two year term. Shortly after the conference, I received a letter from a professor named Cecelia Wendler, who indicated she had considered developing and editing a book entitled "The HeArt of Nursing", as a result of the presentations at the workshop. She requested my permission to be able to include the poem Catharsis in that text. I sent my permissions, but retained the rights to reproduce the work in other forms. I did not hear back from her until the next conference which was held the following year.

As Eta Psi Chapter President, I was expected to attend that next conference to represent our Chapter and be present to vote in the House of Delegates. Another invitation was sent out to STTI members to submit applications for a second HeArt of Nursing display. I again submitted material and it was again chosen for display. I was able to actually meet Dr. Wendler at this conference as she attended it as a presenter. She indicated she would like to include a second poem I had written in the text she was developing. I was very pleased with this request and when the book was published the following year the two poems were included within its pages. A second hard back edition was later published and my poems were in that text as well.

Another success that our chapter achieved was for the acknowledgement of work that was done at a homeless shelter in the Asheville area of establishing a nurses clinic which evaluated and supported wellness. There was a lot of work done by volunteer nurses at this shelter and it was validating to have received the acknowledgement for the efforts that had been made.

Chapter Twenty-one
Return to Work in the Shifting Dynamics of Health Care

After I finished the BSN program I worked for a short time in a temporary position with Professor Carol Stevens, as she was developing the Masters in Nursing program. This was a unique role and experience which placed me close to nurses in the Western Carolina Nursing Community.

I enjoyed and appreciated this contact and feel like it added to my knowledge and understanding of professional and academic nursing positions and responsibilities. I also enjoyed the comradely feelings that I experienced during those months while working at WCU.

I then began applying to different Psychiatric units and hospitals within the area. I was hired at Appalachian Hall an offshoot of Psychiatric Institutes of America in a part time position. A short while later I also took a position at Bridgeway Treatment Center in Brevard. I gained additional experience in mental health with an emphasis on substance abuse treatment from Bridgeway. Appalachian Hall reflected a broad application of Psychiatric treatment's and the facility housed and treated a patient population with broad spectrum of diagnosis and age differences on its varied floors.

The change in situations that arose for Bridgeway was an end product of the changes in Medicaid and what services would generally be paid for in Mental Health Treatment. Within a matter of two months Bridgeway went from a fully functioning 28 to 30 day treatment program with a census of 40 plus clients to a smaller census of 10 to 12 clients. This resulted in a large reduction of overall staff to just a few nurses and technicians. This census eventually dropped to a daily census of 3 to 4 clients. This was prior to the unit's eventual but complete closure.

With major changes in healthcare payment and fears related to job stability many of the nursing staff quickly resigned. This left a number of nursing positions open and as this hospital was closest to our home I applied for one of the positions. I knew it might be short lived but I liked being able to work close to home on an as needed basis. With my evident psychiatric interest and experience I was hired very quickly.

While working in this position I experienced a particularly difficult bout with depression. The St. Johns Wort had stopped working the year before and I had stopped taking it. I would find out later that this over the counter preparation was helpful for depression for a limited period of time but its benefits fade if used for more than a year.

I approached the chaplain of the hospital, who was also a person who had visited our home during Herbert's illness and decline, and was someone with whom I had developed a trusting relationship. I told him of my need for support. He encouraged me to go for some intervention counseling through the hospitals employee services program. It was an excellent suggestion. This was the first time, in all my years of having bouts with depression that a therapist suggested regular antidepressant medications could be of support and assistance to me.

I was started on Zoloft 25 mg and it was gradually increased to 50 mg. I felt results from the medication, combined with the support of the counseling, within a few weeks of starting the medication. I completed the brief counseling and was tapered off the Zoloft within a year and a half. Things seemed more stable for me for a period of time. I would, however, face other challenges that would again require medication later in my life.

A decision was meanwhile made by the Transylvania Hospital to close Bridgeway as a substance abuse treatment center. A closing ceremony was held and I was asked to provide some poems I had written that addressed the sadness related to the loss of this unit from the community, the clients who had received its valuable care, and the staff who had dedicated long hours and efforts to the support its existence. Those poems, along with an explanation preamble, were later a part of the presentation, which I displayed at the second STTI conference I attended, and they are penned on the following pages.

Bridgeway substance abuse and chemical dependency treatment center, located at Transylvania Community Hospital in Brevard, North Carolina, closed its doors to inpatient treatment in the fall of 1999. Through individual counseling and family therapy it had made a difference in the lives of hundreds of clients in need of substance abuse treatment.

On the last day of its existence the staff and former patients of Bridgeway sadly gathered for a closing ceremony. This closure is one example of the multiple losses and changes healthcare has and is experiencing. Many factors contributed to this end result. Some included the continuing rise in the cost of healthcare, tightening of service manager's budgets, the practice of placing healthcare in for profit markets, often changing political focus on which healthcare issues are currently of the most importance and deserved support, and the sometimes unpredicted crises of the facility in question. In order to survive some healthcare providers had formed numerous corporate ventures, drastically cut nursing positions, trimmed a number of services provided, and as in the case with Bridgeway, some have been forced to close all together.

Nurses share greatly in these multiple losses and changes. Many who have provided understanding, compassionate, and dedicated care through one employer have suddenly found themselves bereft of a sense of stability in the position they fill and fearful of the unknown that lays ahead of them. There is concern if the job is lost it could occur without severance or retirement packages and without time or opportunity for closure on intense feelings or even for opportunities to say simple goodbyes. The heart of nursing has often experienced disappointment, loss, illness, pain and the uncertainty of an unknown future.

This heart should also be allowed, encouraged, and provided the opportunity to participate in the journey to healing. The closure of Bridgeway offered an opportunity for me to express feelings in an artistic manner and to offer support to others who were also going through this change in their lives through the use of this written medium.

<u>BRIDGEWAY</u>

Silence
Where once a hundred voices filled the day
Shadows
Where once the sun shone bright with hope and faith
Tears
At letting go of what was but is no more
Reaching
Hands and hearts to those who came to find themselves
Caring
About each other and ourselves
Supporting
Those who suffer losses in whatever way we can
Smiling
At the good times and the joy of being alive
Turning
Pages in the book of life again
Stepping
One foot first and then another
Healing
Comes in its own form and in its own time
Moving
Forward each in our own directions toward our own destinies
Remembering
Forever what we each found here and those we care about

Josephine McCall

TERMINATION

Draw the shades
Dust the tables and shelves one more time
Stack the books and run your hands across the desk
Touch your memories and think of brighter days gone by
of successes more then failures and
hope that was given to many
where none had been before

Turn off the lights and cross the threshold
Close the door with a steady and firm hand
Stand on the patio and take a deep breath
Take one last look at the past and what use to be
Let the wind dry the tears that flow freely from your eyes
Say a final goodbye to a friend
you will not see again

ENVISIONED

**A gliding sunbeam
Just came through the door
And with its light
Softly touched the floor
A million particles of dust
May now be seen
Reflecting in the bath
Of sunlight's sheen
A sadness touches brow
As I recall
How briefly that it lasts
From start to fall
A glimmer of a hope
For light anew
As daybreak leads the way
To morning dew
Each step that I may take
Is first not last
Until my future
Slowly becomes past
And in the bridge of time
That's in between
I find I remember
Sunlight, dewdrops and
Dreams**

PARTING

A parting message
I would give
A hope for strength
Each day you live
A prayer for knowledge
As you go
An inner Peace
Within you grow
A sense of faith
In all mankind
That trust there will be
For you to find
A reaching out
Of hands to search
To find without
The inner perch
A gentle nature
Guide your path
To answer questions
You would ask
And lead you back
Around again
Ere places that
You've never been

During that same year, and shortly after the closure of Bridgeway, the second treatment facility, Appalachian Hall, where I was employed announced its closure as well. The halls of the facility were emptied within a week and its doors were then closed and sealed. There had been many suspicions that this might happen as there had been news articles on the television of negative occurrences within some of the facilities, but there had been no direct or official warning from management that it would definitely occur. It felt as if the management waited until the very last possible moment to say the closure was happening.

In the two weeks prior to this announcement, I had been in conversation with one of the Physician Assistants who worked at both Appalachian Hall and the Julian F. Keith Alcohol and Drug Abuse Treatment Center in Black Mountain. Wally Sturgis indicated ADATC would be opening a new unit within the next month and I should consider applying for a position as a nurse on this new unit. I applied, and had just completed my interview the day before the announcement was made for plans to close Appalachian Hall. I had already negotiated my schedule and had been accepted for hire, prior to that announcement. I called three of my nurse coworkers, who worked at Appalachian and encouraged them to apply to ADATC. They did so and were immediately hired.

I enjoyed helping to open the new ADATC unit and verbally contracted to work three 12 hour shifts a week from 10 am to 10 pm. As I lived an hour away, this seemed the best way to serve the unit and make use the best use of my own time. The unit opened with all of the usual bumps and difficulties that would be expected with this type of endeavor. I was able to share from my experience in mental health of the different types of detox regimens I had seen used and to say which ones had seemed to be the most successful. I definitely felt a part of this team as it developed over the course of the next few months.

After the first year and half, I was approached by the Director of Nursing. She indicated to me that my initial verbal contract for 12 hour shifts would have to change. I would be working 10 hour shifts 4 days a week, at the same hourly rate, due to the units change in needs. I still felt this was a reasonable arrangement and I gave no disagreement to the change even though I would be leaving work a little later at 11 pm at night. I felt a little disgruntled, but it was not worth making it an issue.

One afternoon, I got a call from my mother-in-law, and my Mother was being taken to the hospital in Sylva, as she had apparently had symptoms of a heart attack. I left work and was there at the hospital by the time the ambulance arrived. Mother had a severe heart attack, and between my sister and I, we decided it would be best for Mother to be able to return to Asheville. With this arrangement she could live with, and be cared for, by my sister and be closer to emergency medical care if and when it was needed. Mothers move back to Asheville was made when she was discharged from the hospital. My brother Eddie also returned to Asheville in what turned out to be a temporary basis.

Within the next 6 months, the DON at ADATC again approached me, to say I would have to change to 8 hour shifts, 5 days a week, coming in at 3:30 pm and leaving between 11:30 and 12 midnight. I did point out that this was a big change from the initial agreement and it would place me driving a long distance 5 days a week and I would not be getting home until the early morning hours. I was presented with the option of making the change, or consider leaving the employment, as this was what was needed for the facility. The pay was good and I liked both the work and the easy working relationship I had with my coworkers, so I chose to stay.

One particular night in the early winter, I left work close to 12 midnight. The temperature was not as yet at freezing and I did not anticipate any problems in getting home. As I rounded a curve about 30 minutes from home and placed my foot on the brake of the truck I was driving, I slid off the road. The truck downed a fence and landed on its left side in a field. The driver's door and window were snug against the ground. I could not get out from the position I was in and began to honk the horn loudly. It took several minutes before someone from a trailer down the road heard the sound and called for assistance from the closest fire department. The firemen placed a number of hands on the truck to steady it and had me to climb out the door of the truck as they held it open and steadied the truck. They were very concerned it might flip on its top when I started to get out. I had been fortunate that it had not turned completely over when it spun off the highway on the black ice which could have caused me to be seriously injured.

Thankfully I only had physical bruising from the accident and I had been able to contact my husband to come to the scene. He was then able to take me home and the truck was actually drivable, once it was pulled from the field. The next day, I was physically stiff and sore but that result of the accident passed quickly. What did not pass was the anxiety and depression that can sometimes result from such an accident. I seemed to find myself less and less able to make the long trip to and from the unit, or to be able to stay focused on my work. I felt locked into the situation and unable to deal with how I was feeling. I needed some time and distance away from the job to evaluate the situation, but did not feel I would be given this time off if I asked for it from management.

One of the nurses I worked with suggested I see my family physician who could indicate a request for me to take a leave of absence from work. This would give me the time I needed to deal with the emotional results of the previous accident and I could request that the physician consider placing me back on an antidepressant. The possibility of some relief helped to give me hope and this was the course I took. In addition to ordering me to take a leave of absence, my physician did put me back on the antidepressant I had previously been taking, to treat the depression.

It took 2 weeks for the depression to begin to lift, during which I hibernated in my husband and my bedroom and spoke only to him and when I had to. When the medication began to help, it was like someone turned on a light switch and I again felt like breathing and living. At the end of that month, I made the difficult decision to resign from my position at ADATC and gave a month's notice in the resignation. This allowed time for the facility to find a replacement for my position and for me to say goodbyes.

With minor alterations, I have remained on an antidepressant to the present.

I also learned that individuals who have experienced childhood abuse may not have as much circulating serotonin in their systems and this can be a major cause or support for their depression. They may also experience an exacerbation of a condition named Post Traumatic Stress Disorder if they are faced with intense and stressful situations. The medication that has been most effective for me has been what is referred to as a Selective Serotonin Reuptake Inhibitor. I was grateful for the help and willing to be open to learning as I went. There are long term studies that discuss the way serotonin receptors develop and there is a premise they develop differently in individuals who experience trauma when they are young.

I had made many friends at ADATC and knew I would miss them sorely. Sometimes, it is not only the pay or the benefits that holds us as nurses to a position. It is also the service you can provide to your client population and the interactions with the staff with whom you work that will make the difference in whether you stay or leave a job.

One of my coworkers was a nurse named Judy Keels. It was apparent she had a lot of experience in working with the substance abuse population and was very good in the position she filled. During our months of working together, I felt I had learned a good deal from her and I really liked her as a nurse and as a person. She was one of the individuals to whom it would be hard to say goodbye. She had always been supportive of my work and my growth in this setting.

At one point during our working relationship, Judy had gone through a difficult time trying to provide support to a couple who were friends of hers. The husband was slowly dying of cancer and Judy was providing support for both the husband and the wife, in addition she was trying to deal with her own knowledge that she herself was losing a friend. I felt such empathy for her that I tried to find a way to give her some type of support in the task she was trying to achieve. As is often the case, I tried to write something that might help. The following is the piece I wrote and dedicate to her. She stated it was of help to her and I so hoped that was the case.

Bereaved

I will walk with you through this change in the focus of our lives.

I will hold your hand and give to you from my heart and faith all that I have to give.

I will love you and share with you laughter, memories and tears.

We can talk of successes and failures, the joys and challenges of raising children, and what we feel has been most important to each of us in life.

When there is the need I will take you in my arms and hold you to me and let you cry as I cry with you.

When you are in pain I will do all that I can to provide you with comfort.

If you become tired I will encourage you to rest. I will turn the lights down and spend time with you quietly.
When you reach the point where you are ready and feel it is time to go I will walk with you to the threshold that separates life and death.

With tears of grieving I will say a sad good-bye and although it may be the hardest thing I've had to do in this life I will allow you the space you need to take that final step.

For you see I love you and I know that I must let you go.

Josephine McCall

(Dedicated to Judy Keels for all the caring and sharing you have done in and with your life. You are a true friend and dedicated soul and you have been a model to others in your thoughts, actions and dedication to all within your space.)

After I left employment at the ADATC, I spent some time assisting in my mother-in-laws medical care, as she was having on-going cardiac problems and later frequent knee surgeries. For a time, Pauline was a patient at Transylvania Hospital, where I had worked on the Bridgeway unit as an RN.

While there with her, I ran into a former coworker, who told me of a job that was available at a local girl's camp, as a nurse for the summer. This was two days after I had left employment at ADATC. I called and made an appointment and was interviewed for a position at Rockbrook Camp for Girls the next day. I liked the owner of the camp, Jerry Stone, and could sense the positive team work that went on among this group of professionals. I was offered a job that day.

This situation offered me an opportunity to work in a positive atmosphere with people who were upbeat and energetic. The staff also had a healthy approach to caring for and working with girls from a young age to adulthood, and provided support and education through the use of numerous physically and challenging activities. The staff also addressed spiritual issues without differentiating religious difference which is such an important and balanced approach that can be taken in life. We all live in this world together regardless of what faith we choose to live within. Rockbrook's philosophy of acceptance was reflected by those who worked and resided there.

This was the first time I had experienced working at a camp and I felt blessed to have the chance to be there. I have worked many summers at this camp after being employed that first year. I wrote some poetry that the owner later asked me to read at one of the campsites fireside programs and I was pleased to be able to share it there.

Rockbrook

I quietly climb the mossy rocks beside the silvered stream
I stop and gaze at the waterfall as droplets splatter on the grassy banks
I swirl upwards, past the campfire, through the pines
and hemlocks that are swaying wispy branches as I go
I watch as the morning mist rises slowly from the
ground to the sky
I see the sparkle of dewdrops as they cling to the petals
of the flowers and plants below

I dive to the middle of the lake and see the ripples
dance across the water and know
these small swells wash upon the shores of many
different times and places
I take wing and soar with the birds to a spot where they
hover at the top of the
evergreen trees
The world around me breaths out an expectant sigh
and pauses on the threshold of one nights ending and
another days new beginning
I wait with anticipation and joy in my soul for the birth
of this new day

Mountain Spirit Guide

I am as old as the trees around me and as young as the tiniest feet
that patter across these pine needle floors
I am the hope of spring and new life and the warming memories
thought of on a cold winters night
I am the smell of flowers, roasting hotdogs, campfire smoke, and
liniment salve
I am the silence of a restful sleep and the noise of a happy
mealtime
I am the firefly light on a dark and moonless night and the colors
of the rainbow seen through a fine spray mist on a hot dry day
I am the healing and acceptance of illness and a peaceful
resolution
to conflict
I am the joy of friendship and sharing and the bittersweet sadness
of farewell
I am the sense of maturity that comes from taking the chances
life has to offer and the satisfaction of knowing I have done
what was right

Josephine McCall

I am strong but gentle and caring
I often lead but can also follow
I am a thread in the fiber of life and a part of each of those who walk the mountain trails and seek to know themselves
I am a mountain spirit guide and will survive as long as one person remembers how to seek me out

In the fall of 2003, I interviewed for an RN position with Smoky Mountain Center for a new crises stabilization unit that was opening January of the following year. I was hired into that position, along with 5 other nurses. I continued in that employment as a full time and then a PRN nurse, until December of 2009.

Along with working at the Smoky Mountain Center Balsam Adult Recovery Unit in 2001 my husband and I opened a small plant nursery, near Waynesville. The nursery was situated next to the Pigeon River, in Lake Junaluska, North Carolina. We developed and ran this nursery for three years.

At the same time we were building the nursery, Kenneth and his brother made trips to Tennessee, to seek out resources for some of the plants we might want to raise and sell. They had found some land in a little place called Altamont, Tennessee, and Kenneth spoke for a couple of acres of property in a small area on Gap Road.

It was a very quiet and rural piece of land in a beautiful part of Grundy County. Kenneth and Curtis, along with other projects, set about building us a house on the property. When it was finished, for a time it came to be mine and Kenneth's place of Solace where we could get away from home, family and everyday stress. I would say it was some of the best times we had together and spoke of private space and a better future for the both of us. I can say we were both content when we were there and that was a tangible and wonderful feeling.

In 2004, I was approached by a nurse that I had known from the Tuberculosis Sanitarium, who had later become an instructor in the nursing program at Haywood Community College in Waynesville, NC. She asked me if I would be interested in becoming a clinical instructor for nursing students in the mental health setting where I worked.

This position would be two days a week for the once a year semester in which mental health was taught. It sounded interesting, the pay was comparable, and I was already in a position where I could make choices about my unit and work schedule. The Nurse Manager, Marcia Parlier, at the Balsam Center was very supportive of the idea of having someone who worked at the unit being involved with the students in this manner. I appreciated that consideration greatly. I took the offer and stayed in that position through the fall of 2009. It became a wonderful way to give back to others some of the experience I had gained along the way. I enjoyed watching as students in the clinical area learned as much about themselves, as they learned about the subject and nature of mental health.

During the fall of 2004, people in Haywood, Buncombe and Jackson County, were hit with 2 floods, back to back, secondary to Hurricanes Ivan and Francis. The water rose inside our nursery building up to 21 inches with the first flood and 29 inches with the second. It destroyed everything in the building and most of our nursery stock within the nursery property. The stock had been covered with flood waters contaminated with sewage and oil waste water. Even with government assistance that was provided secondary to our loss of inventory, we were never able to recover from all our losses. The help did keep us from totally sinking as a family and as farmers. It also allowed us to be able to pay off the balance on the land we had purchased in Haywood County and on which we established the nursery. With much sadness, we were eventually forced to close this nursery lot and another chapter in our lives.

While working on the Adult Recovery Unit I would, when

it was appropriate, and with the physicians permission, share some of my writings with clients. I also shared with staff when it was requested and if it seemed it would help someone in his or her movement toward healing. It appeared to be validating for the individual who was reading the work, and provided validation for me as a person that hearing about recovery can be helpful to others. Life stayed busy and Kenneth was in the process of starting to build a log home on the property at Pin Hook, that he said would be where we would retire to when we were a little older.

In 2006, two outstanding events occurred that would affect our lives in a major way. We received word from a neighbor in Tennessee that our house had caught fire the night before and had basically burned to the ground. There had been a severe thunder storm the previous night and the house had apparently been struck by lightning. I was in the clinical area with students when I got the call from Kenneth. I was devastated to think of the loss. We were fortunate as we did have insurance, but that could never replace what had come to be a special place of retreat for the both of us. The money from that house and those belongings would help on the current construction of the log home in Pin Hook, but I would never see it as an equitable tradeoff. We lost more than a house as a result of that fire. We would never again be able to recapture that sense of peace, happiness and freedom the house had afforded us.

The second event occurred a number of months later as I began experiencing occasional headaches and lightheadedness. This lasted over several weeks.

One morning when the headache was intense, I asked the Physician's Assistant who made rounds on our unit to check my blood pressure. David Lyle was a PA and an excellent example of a medical provider. He was very concerned when he found it was elevated at 220/118. I again had students in the clinical area that day and indicated to him I would get it checked by my physician as soon as possible. In hindsight, I probably should have tried to find coverage for the students, or sent them home then gone on to the physician's office, but I choose to wait. I was able to be seen later that afternoon by my medical provider. She made a number of changes in my prescription medications and over the next 2 weeks, my BP gradually decreased to a more normal level. This was the proverbial wake up call for me. I decided if there were things in life I wanted to do, that I needed to make steps in those directions. Life does not always wait for what each of us may want to accomplish.

One of the first things I did was to consider writing a book related to my recovery from the childhood issues I experienced. I received a lot of support for this idea and I started this manuscript within the next few months.

In 2007, I was encouraged by a close friend to return to nursing school to obtain my Masters of Science in Nursing Education. Rod and I had known each other for a number of years, had worked together at ADATC, and then again for a time at the Balsam Center. We had often teased back and forth about returning to school to obtain our Master of Science in Nursing Degrees. At first, I did not take it as a serious consideration or real possibility but, with continued encouragement and recognizing this would be something I would do for me, I finally began taking initial steps in that direction.

I was also again dealing with a number of stresses that had arisen between my husband and myself. I saw applying for school as an interest that would distract me from the changing environment at home, where I did not seem to be a part of what was taking place. School could also be a way of providing for my own emotional needs. I thought it would take a number of try's to pass the Graduate Record Evaluation, which is a required test to get into the program. If that was the case, I would have some time to more easily work my way into the position of returning to school. I filled out the initial application for the MSN program and moved on to the next step. Acceptance into the MSN program would partially depend on the results of the GRE and I thought that step would probably be a prolonged to little later in my future.

With the many hours I was working at that time, I was not able to study more than a day or so prior to that test. I was shocked a few weeks later, to find I had passed high enough on the first test attempt, to be accepted into WCU's MSN program. I sent all the official documents and paperwork that were required and I was notified of my acceptance for the following fall. I then applied for scholarships, some of which I also received.

I was excited and anxious at the same time when I started into 3 online classes with Western and a night statistics class at Haywood Community college. With 3 jobs and school, I was on overload. The situation with my husband and home life also continued to deteriorate and it seemed like I was constantly trying to deal with one personal crisis after another. I dropped one of the Western courses and simply hung in there with the rest. I passed the three classes with decent grades and wiped the sweat from my forehead, then asked myself what it was going to take to lighten the load under which I had found myself. Experiences at home were beginning to tear me apart emotionally. I was simply overwhelmed.

I took one more semester of 2 classes at Western, before it became necessary for me to stop the process of continuing my education for an unspecified period of time. The marital relationship fractured and life again took a major shift with which I needed to deal. I think part of that shift was the result of the growth that had taken place through the initial writing of this book, part was my recognizing that life at home had taken a possibly irreversible shift, and my recognizing I had a need to again make changes, in which my husband was either unwilling or unable to participate.

Regardless of all the specifics, it took me 1 ½ years of painful emotional work and intense support from close friends and counselors to find my way through the depression and turmoil that had resulted from the broad number of challenges I faced and went through. I have come to understand I will continue to grieve over this loss until I reach some measure of peace and closure on this part of my past.

To have made the statement I had reached a state of healing when I was not fully convinced that was true, became an important issue for me. It was time to again look in the mirror and see what else it would take to make that an honest and soul felt reflection. I made, and continue to make those steps, for I have learned, if nothing else, that healing and recovery are ongoing processes with many rises and falls along the way. I am daily in recovery from a past life and find the steps forward taking each day as it comes are made with increasing strength and a sense of faith in this life I have been fortunate enough to live.

Developing an awareness of my own needs helped me to move forward. Being able to process issues that occurred when I was a child and then addressing the behaviors and feelings that resulted has allowed me to have a happier and more beneficial existence. In the later part of my life, I recognized that healing and recovery from pain is not a closed ended experience and that I have to be cognizant of what is occurring within me, to keep me on that life long journey. This has given me the stability and insight that I needed in order to provide appropriate and compassionate care to those to whom I am accountable and to the spirit that lives within us all.

I have learned there is among our nursing family, support to be given and obtained. As nurses, we do not have to feel competitive, threatened by concepts we do not understand, fearful of constructive criticism, or incompetent in what we do. We do not, as the saying goes, have to eat our young. We can all find ways to be a team player and work together for the good of us all as providers and receivers of care. Part of that ability is to recognize the needs of ourselves, our coworkers, and our clients and then be willing to ask the right questions. We can then give helpful support. I encourage anyone who reads this book who has left over pain from a traumatic past, to move forward to the better and happier life that waits for those who are willing to try.

PETALS FROM THE MASTERS BOUQUET

A collection of poems and other works

The Masters Bouquet

The Master took his calloused hands
And scattered star dust ore the land
With a thought he blossomed flowers
From the ground
Then the swirls of colors came
To each he gave a name
And granted that the world would share
In a Masters Bouquet

Trans-illusion

(Picture in your mind you have received a card and a candle in the mail, and on the card it says:)

As the cold winds of November and December swirl around your door
Light this candle
And as the smoke sends spirals to the ceiling
Let your worries and your cares rise with them
Then let you mind drift to a more peaceful time
In the future or in the past
And let your mind drift to a more Peaceful time
Either in the future or in the past
And let your whole being be attuned to this one moment
Of Peace and Harmony

Guardian of Spring

A specter rises from the river's edge
With long and flowing hair she gently glides across the rising mist
She is a slender form
With beaded sideburns braids and skin that might have been an olive tan
In grace she lights upon the ground
With almost wispy fingers she touches budding flowers on their stem
Dewdrops weep from petals in her stride
She places hand to brow
With eyes that were a deep and piercing brown she surveys all in view

She fades into the shadows at a moment's breath
She waves her hand and breezes softly follow in her lead
She sighs and melody cascades a thousand tiny chimes
She cries and raindrops warmly bathe the land
She firmly touches timber and wills for it to grow, it's time
She is angry and a storm burst through the clouds
She cannot leave this valley for this is home
And lonely though she sometimes is
She thinks of when the world was new and young
She smiles and sunbeams dance across the sky
She is the Indian maiden chosen Guardian of Spring

A NURSE'S PRAYER

(Written shortly after the 911 disaster)

CREATOR,
WE STAND HERE BEFORE YOU AS A PEOPLE OF MANY NATION'S, MANY CULTURE'S, MANY CREED'S AND BELIEF'S. WE EACH VIEW YOU IN OUR OWN INDIVIDUAL AND PERSONAL WAY.

WE WHO ARE NURSES HAVE SEEN MIRACLES IN PROGRESS AND HAVE OFTEN SEEN THE POWER OF ANSWERED PRAYERS. THE COUNTRY WHEREIN WE STAND AND THE FOUNDATIONS ON WHICH IT WAS ESTABLISHED HAVE BEEN ATTACKED. THE RESULT WAS PAIN AND GREVIOUS LOSS. THIS COUNTRY AND ITS DIFFERING FAITHS AND PATHS IS NOT THE FIRST TO EXPERIENCE SUCH AN

ATTACK AND IS NOT LIKELY FOR A TIME TO BE THE LAST. THE EXPERIENCE HAS AT SOME LEVEL TOUCHED ALL THAT LIVE WITHIN ITS BOUNDARIES AND MANY WHO LIVE THROUGHOUT THE WORLD. A ONE TIME SENSE OF TOTAL SAFETY HAS NOW BEEN REPLACED WITH NECESSARY CAUTION.

WE AS NURSES AND HEALERS HAVE ALWAYS AND WILL CONTIUNE TO GRIEVE FOR THE PAIN, SUFFERING, AND DEATH OF INNOCENTS AND AFFLICTED PEOPLES. WE HAVE ALWAYS MINISTERED TO THOSE IN NEED. IT IS HOWEVER WE WHO ARE NOW AND AT THIS TIME AMONG THOSE WHO NEED TO HEAL. WE AS NURSES SEEK SPIRITUAL HEALING AND GUIDANCE AS WE LOOK TOWARD THE HOPE THAT STEPS WE TAKE FORWARD FROM HERE ARE TOWARD THE HEALING OF OURSELVES, OUR SOULS, AND IN SOME WAY THROUGH OUR PROFESSION AND HANDS WE CAN HELP IN THE HEALING OF ALL MANKIND.

WE ARE AWARE WITH SPIRITUAL GUIDANCE AND SUPPORT THAT WE AS NURSE'S MAKE A DIFFERENCE IN THE LIVES OF OTHERS WHERE EVER WE MAY LIVE.

Balance

I will each day give myself time and space
to seek the center of my soul
I will draw to myself positive energy and move
daily toward Peace and happiness
I will today learn what it takes for me
to maintain at a healthy state
In so doing I will acknowledge the abundance
of joy that life has to offer and attempt to learn
from the varied challenges with which I have been blessed
I will climb beyond the demands of everyday life
and recognize the shades of my own aura
I will then be able to accept the boundaries and the varied
hues of light that surrounds those with whom I live this day
From this perspective I can then provide balanced support
and have the potential to share with others from the lessons I have
learned this day

Mid-Line Time-Line Just so fine

In a time before knowing what tomorrow may bring
We take and make the best we can of today
Before being told of a child's massive inabilities, of a friends sudden demise
Of a spouse's incurable disease, of the loss of a home, job or way of life, of
Some catastrophe that will forever change our established view of how our lives have
Been or what they might become

Before any major happening of the distant future, the next hour or minute

This means we hold in our hands the happiness of nowI treasure the knowing of now and the not knowing of tomorrow
It gives me time to appreciate the life I have so that I do not dwell on the negatives of what
May be in the crystal ball of tomorrow or the next few years, days or hours

Introduction

Christmas is supposed to be one of the most joyous seasons of the year, but that is not always the case, if there has been a loss of someone you love and care for. This note is to acknowledge that love does not vanish with the loved one's death and especially the first holidays without them are sometimes the hardest to get through. Know that family and friends around you are aware of these feelings and are there with open arms to share this difficult time with you. May you have the best possible outcome for you and yours during this holiday season.

Suppositions

You were supposed to cut the turkey, say the blessings, help wrap
the presents, help decorate the tree, and make the many memories
that come with Christmas time.
You were supposed to spend the rest of your life with me and help
to spoil the grandchildren that aren't even here yet.

Josephine McCall

You were supposed to come back to me whole and hardy and we
would start the holiday season together like we have for years.
But somehow this time you didn't make the circle and I'm left
here without you.
How can I say the thousands of words to you that I meant to but
never got around to saying?
How can I hear all the things you intended to say but never said?
If I find a shirt you tossed in the corner of the closet will the scent
make you stand close beside me if for only that moment?
If I think the words I love you will you hear them, if I listen
closely will I still hear your voice talking to me in the night?
If I write you a letter in the sand will you see it before the tide
takes it away?
If I hold your love close to me will it keep me safe and help me get
through the miles ahead that I had not planned to travel alone?
I hope so, for that faith, your memories, and our children is what I
have left to remind me of you and to help me take the steps I must
take.

Breana (granddaughter)

You are your mother's soul and your father's heart
with the crinkle of your eyes you have them in the palm of your
hands
You will often achieve whatever it is your young mind has
thought of at that moment with no more action then the
blink of your mischievous eyes

Josephine McCall

Brilliant and bubbly you sparkle like a comet flying in
the midnight sky
With your hair ablaze and the colors of a brilliant evening
sunset and a smile on your face warm enough to melt
mountains of snow
Situated at your eye level you stretch to peer over the kitchen table
and look beyond, through the windows, to the wide world that
awaits you. You hesitate only a moment and then your off
again, with energy to spare, chasing whatever is available to
catch even if it's only the focus of your grandfathers attention

I was in a situation where a child was being chastised in what could have been considered a demeaning manner. It made me think of how such interventions done with the best of intentions at such a tender age can have long term negative effects on a child. As this child is close to my heart, I tried to think of a way to say my thoughts, that would not come across in an unfeeling or threatening manner. I definitely wanted to be heard, so I generalized in my approach.

The following is written with the consideration of children often being at the mercy of those who care for them.

In Your Hands

In your hands you cradle the fragile wings of innocence and the molten clay of a young child's hopes and dreams for the future. If shaped by hands that exhibit acceptance, consideration, realistic limits and expectations, respect, generosity of spirit and unconditional love.

This child could grow strong and learn to have faith in his or her self and in those who are around him or her. He or she is likely to live a full and productive life filled with joy and hope with a balanced respect for taking risk instead of a grudging fear.

This can result in knowledge and acceptance of life as something to be experienced in a positive way. From this gift of security this child may grow to be inspired and independent and then could lead others by example.

By nature he or she will care and share with others all that has been learned and his or her spirit could have the opportunity to soar with the wind and rise to the stars.

If shaped by hands that exhibit intolerance, anger, rigid control and dominance, unrealistic and self-centered expectations, belittling, and love provided with numerous conditions, this child could grow to be afraid of the world around him or her, to associate love with pain and distrust, to never be sure of his or herself or be able to develop a secure sense of self separate from others.
He or she may always question any decisions made and could feel nothing that is done is ever worthwhile or good enough.

From this gift of insecurity, he or she may become a victim of those who sense such frailty, lack of stability, and poor sense of self.

By nature, he or she may be withdrawn and shy, his or her spirit may ever flutter close to the safety of the ground and then may fear to climb the lofty heights that hover above them.

Negative lessons learned as a young child can take a whole lifetime to unlearn and faith in self may only be gained in the sacrifice of self.

For the sake of children, it behooves us all to recognize how and what we are teaching by word, but also important, is what we teach by example, during the precious time we have make a difference to a child.

Chaos

My mind is empty of congruent thoughts
lines that crisscross and run together
with no barriers to slow them down
If they stop I would probably lose my sanity
because I would then have to acknowledge how really
close to the edge of infinity we both are

Strands

If will could make you stronger you would be hale and hardy
Your faith in life has been strong, as is mine
But life does not always respond to what each of us,
as individuals, hope for the most
So you and I must take our steps one at a time
and not look so much toward the morrow
but gently grasp around our fingers the single strands of fiber
that woven together
make up today
I will respect and abide by the choices you have made
you have the right to choose,
how you live and when illness has become too hard and
you feel it is time for you to let go and to die
I love you and always have
I will support you as best I can through these final steps and
into the transition you are now choosing to make

I worked with a friend who is a little younger than me and she had four adult children one of whom was a son in his twenties. She received word that one of her son had been unexpectedly killed when the motorcycle he was riding was hit by a car. It was obvious and understandable that she was devastated by the news. Those around her tried to provide what support they could, but we all knew that for her, this would be a long and painful journey.

I tried to put myself in her shoes and wrote the following reflections. I paired the piece with a scrap book that had many unfilled pages. Later, when a little time had passed, I gave her the book and the written note. I told her that someday, when she felt able, she would fill this book with memories of all the wonderful things she knew about and shared with her son. I wished her healing in her own time and in her own way.

She had an opportunity thrust upon her a few months later, when she had some unexpected surgery and was forced to take some time off from work. She had much time to herself during that period and she made some major choices about a different direction she wanted her life to take. She also allowed herself to do some initial grieving. I have not heard from her much since she left us and ventured forward into this different phase of her nursing career, but the last time I saw her, she seemed much more on her way to healing than previously.

Death, and the resulting grief can be so overwhelming that it feels like you cannot breath. I can only hope that reading or hearing words that validate our losses and feelings can be of the kind of support that is useful and may be needed when in this state of pain.

Unexpected

**My soul is heavy laden
the grief feels like more than I can ever bare
You have gone from us without warning
my mind has been told you have left but
My heart cannot accept this loss
I reach for the phone to call you
How do I tell my hand to stop in this movement
I think of your beginning and I cry
The twinkle in your eyes
the energy in your step
your hopes and dreams as you grew
all that you became
How do I let you go**

Reunions Dedicated to Erwin High School Graduates Class of 1968

Childhood forward

Large black and white TV's gave way to color, with receivers the size of a wristwatch. Eventually, you could watch movies at home with Betas, then VHS and now DVD players. Computers went from the size of large rooms, to laptops and palm sized multifunctional telephones that interface with satellites', 33 1/3 records evolved to 8 track tapes, then cassettes, then cd's and IPods. Human manned spaceships went from unmanned science fiction to space station science fact, but not without a number of human losses along the way.

Some of our birthing cries were heard around the time of the Korean War, which was later followed by Vietnam, The Gulf War, the shock and outrage of Sept 11th, then the most recent conflicts in Afghanistan and the War in Iraq. We hoped wars would stop, but that doesn't seem to be the case for many graduating class. We've lost classmates, friends and relatives in the many conflicts.

As our childhood happened, we watched and listened on the radio, as Elvis the pelvis sang songs like, love me Tender and later as the Beatles took over the airways. Then we heard as our youngest President was first shot, then died in a Texas town. The world joined us as we watched a rider less horse, with boots turned backwards in the stirrups, lead our nation in mourning and a child named John. John saluted at his father's grave.

Who knew that our young prince would one day die in his prime on a foggy night not fit for flying.

In high school, Civil rights was a major issue and some religious leaders paid the ultimate price to be heard. Clyde A Erwin integrated quietly with one young, quiet, brave black girl, who led the way. Another Kennedy lost his life, when he tried to ascend to the White House. He and his brother are still remembered and revered. The last brother of that family now fights his own battle with cancer, but regardless, he has been able to achieve a long and productive political life to the present.

During Physical Education classes, we had our first dances with members of the opposite sex. We wondered wide eyed what fearful or exciting experiences lay ahead for us with the opposite sex, in the unknown and private area of our life. Perhaps too soon, that veil of knowledge was lifted. Perhaps not, after all, school and life were about learning.

The cold war eventually gave way to changes in Russia, splintering its holdings, then the Berlin Wall fell. We raced to cross that threshold, from teenager into adulthood, learning (or trying to learn) Algebra and Geometry, Spanish and French as our new languages. We had choices to make. Clubs and Drama classes, along with Chorus, Band and sports. These rounded out many of our lives. In the 10th, 11th and 125h grade, some of us started with part time jobs and felt the freedom and benefits of having our own money in our hands.

Our parents watched in horror as Haete Ashbury and later, Woodstock happened in foreign places like California and blazed the newspaper and TV. How could they protect us from this immoral invasion of which they had no control? Jr. and Sr. proms came and went.

The school lost excellent teaches when the Steele's were asked to leave for their choices of non belief. Private beliefs are questions that cannot now be broached in interviews. Graduation came and is now a long ago memory and we have since had children and grandchildren of our own, built homes, made commitments and reached a point of a certain since of satisfaction in what we have accomplished along the way.

We've experienced many losses along the way classmates, friends, family. We were blessed to know them and have them in our lives for a time. We have been given the opportunity to live, hope, try, succeed and know we have made a difference in the lives of those around us. We have done more than survived, we have made this a better place to live.

Mixed Works

Son

And you are my child
Tall and blonde
With your fathers hair
And eyes as blue as the sky

No longer babe
But not quite man
You stand beside me, towering already
Reaching for the sun
Your knowledge goes beyond your years
There are times you have had to understand so much
And perhaps too soon
You'll be gone, grown

Josephine McCall

Gifts to you
To cope, to love, to share
I would give you
But you'll find them on your own

Some choices already
My pride in you is great
And I love you
My son

Bittersweet

The cup of life I sip upon
Awakenings to shapes unseen before
Through star glazed eyes

Fall

I stand beneath the tree of life
The wind blows lightly through my hair
Its fall again
And ever so gently
I catch the leafs of gold

Sunlight

Sunlight just crossed the mountain top
And softly placed its hands upon the trees
And in the reverence that I sometimes feel
I find that I am humbled on my knees
For every grey and dusky morn
you will find a patch of blue
For every time I need a friend
I hope to find someone like you

Josephine McCall

Autumn

Fall has come
And leafs of red and gold
Have gently
Wept upon the ground

Salutation

Take care
Walk softly
Be aware
And have faith

Vision

Eyes of wisdom
So they say
But these are things
I should have known
Long before yesterday

Josephine McCall

I Remember

**A gliding sunbeam
Just came through the door
And with its light
Softly touched the floor**

**A million particles of dust
May now be seen
Reflecting in the bath
Of sunlight's sheen**

**A sadness touches brow
As I recall
How briefly that it lasts
From start to fall**

**A glimmer of a hope
For light anew
As daybreak leads the way
To morning dew**

**Each step that I may take
Is first not last
Until my future
Slowly becomes past**

**And in the bridge of time
That's in between
I find I remember
Sunlight, dewdrops and Dreams**

Alternatives

Do not be afraid of me
For you are inspiration
Through your eyes
I see the world
In a different hue

Hope

Travel with me
And I'll take you to the stars
Have faith
And all you wish for can be yours

Winds

Blow lightly autumn winds
For I am not ready
In my hand
The blossom still survives

Ruminations

Bluesy feel and tone down skin
Tiny bridges for many gaps
You are my destiny
If I will but touch your face
Through the looking glass
Ask Alice she knows
she's been where I am going
Put the body to bed, the mind to rest
Tomorrow open other doors
To Past present and gently
To the future
Be patient with me
For I learn slowly
But once aware, I know forever
Tap the drums, lightly
Hear the beat, feel the heat
Through your soul
Taste with open mouth

Reminiscent

It's raining outside
And it makes me think of you
And the warmth we shared
And the warmth I feel
When I think of you
Seems I often
Think of you

Friend

It conjures up a vision of many things
Friend
Someone to share your closest moments with
Your best and your worst
Someone who makes no demands, requires no bonds
But always seems to understand
Friend
Someone who passes no judgments'
Regardless of what others think
Friends
Come in different shapes and sizes, colors and languages
Beliefs and creeds
Friend
Someone to hold near to heart, value and treasure,
And never take for granted
Friend
You are this to me
And I would always have you be
My friend

Consumed

You reach within
and touch the fibers of my soul
You softly, gently, unleash the woman that I am
The inferno that lies below is known to few
But when ignited by your flame
I am consumed.

Blaze

Hands
Reaching to the corner of your eye
Graze your face
And travel down your neck
A pause
As eyes look to eyes
And slowly
Lips join and fire begins
Tenders first
Then flames to a blaze
As two become one
Melded together

Confined

I am a prisoner of my own memories
And quietly cry as they file past
For my review

Background for regrets

Finger to nose
Nose to glass
Eyes full of tears
Toys too far to reach
Christmas here again
Baby's got to wait
Bills to pay
Food to buy

as years go by
Other needs never met
Don't forget
But put to side
Silly pride
Handouts from the higher ups
Grovel some
Ah does the low man on the totem pole
Ever find his way out anyway
Some say
Have to pay
Piper play

Adieu

A wine glass
For the end of a long day and a quiet moment to look forward to
A candle
For the warmth and closeness of friendship glowing in the night
A Basket
For the little things and to represent the hopes and dreams we hope to fulfill
A flower
For the cycle of Life and our each coming to blossom in our own time and in our own special way
And my love
To draw upon like water from a well when you are thirsty

Tiny

Tiny paws upon the door
Tiny patters across the floor
Tiny heartbeats within her breast
Tiny snores as she would rest
Tiny ears that perked with sound
Tiny jumps and leaps and bounds
Tiny love from the very start
Tiny's gone
And took a piece of my heart

Tidbit

Two little blue eyes
Looking at me
Four little paws
Clinging desperately
A tiny cold nose
Thrust against my face
A bunch of little whiskers
All over the place
A crooked little tail
Broken in a fall
A tiny little body
Just barely an inch tall
Soft, fuzzy fur
Nestled in my hand
A steady purring rhythm
Like a small minstrel band
Sweetness of spring
Warmth of summer light

My tiny little tidbit of heaven
Sprung from the cage
Of a dark gloomy night

Love

(Ours) Mine are the flowers
Blossoms in the spring
(Ours) Mine are the cardinals
Voices rise to sing
(Ours) Mine are the rainbows
Colors splashed about
(Ours) Mine are the children
Warmth and care throughout
(Ours) Mine is love

DEATH

I gaze upon the doorway
That leads from here to there
I ask myself some questions
Oh God is it ever fair

The pain the hurt the suffering
The fear that faces all
The things that we must look at
When death comes to call

I shudder and I ponder
Am I ready should it be
My time to cross the threshold
And face eternity

The gate behind me closes
As future becomes past
I wonder, is this the way it is
When we come to breath our last

Dear God, oh to be able
To face this time alone
For there is no way to share it
Between maker and his own

Goodbyes

Soft dark clouds
Overhead

Represent
Tears unshed

Ominous
To the eye

Seems they only
Need to cry

Seasons come
And seasons go

Hard to understand
Them though

Quietly death
Slips through the door

When its time
No one is sure

Harbored angers
Foolish pride

Sometimes makes
Our feelings hide

Kept from making
Our amends

Then we suffer
For our friends

Hard to leave them
Let them go

For we always
Loved them so

Josephine McCall

<u>A closeness across the miles</u>

I walk across the beach
And call your name
And suddenly I feel
You've done the same
A closeness cross the miles
Compassion cries
And look within the depth
Of clear blue skies
A bond that's there between us
I can feel
While on the shores alone now
I do kneel
A friendship born of caring
Within our soul
No need to have you here
Within my hold
A part of you forever
I will be
Just as you'll always be
A part of me
Two people separate
By a bridge of land
But no more then
A simple grain of sand

Reflections

**Where will I be tomorrow
Standing at the golden gates or
Looking at the sands
Chasing rainbows in the sky
Walking hand in hand
Looking at a myriad
Of colors in the trees
Strolling through the flowers
Watching honey bees
Running to the ocean
Splashing in the waves
Kissing tender lips again
Gently holding babes
Packing all my luggage
Traveling abroad
Cradling a notion
Jumping for a ball
Softly viewing candle-light
Sadly shedding tears
Quietly gaining faith again
Fighting all my fears
Gazing to the future
Hoping for the way
Remembering the past
Just as I am today**

Mankind

Gently walk beside
Beside the silver stream
Softly, like you've walked
Within a dream
Touch the withered brow
Of natures soul
Left without a light
It now grows cold
Look beyond the hope
The shroud of man
Deep within the heart
Ambition stands
Furthered by the faith
Of all around
His hopes, his dreams, his plans
Will seek no bounds
Stifled by a sudden
Urge to cry
He finds that he may watch
Another die
And frightened though he is
Of things to come
He knows that there are things
That must be done

Josephine McCall

Nature Center

Clean brisk air
We've gone to the fair
John looks like a clown
Upside down clown
Bills got his candy
Thinks he's a dandy
Saw the girl with the snake
Oh come on! Give me a break
Listened as they played some songs
Decided to sing along
Climbed up on the boardwalk
A niece quiet place to talk
Wandered on the beaten path
Many questions never asked
Watched kids jumping in the hay
Say, I'd sure like to play
Want a bite to eat
Hot dogs and fries are neat
Hey, you got an extra nickel
I want to buy a pickle
Looked at turtle eggs
They do what with their legs??
Ambled past the gentle deer
They didn't even seem to hear
Watched while bees made honey
Set them loose, it might not be funny
Saw the otter
in the water
Bought a pumpkin
With a face
Greens and gold's
All over the place

Spied a squirrel
In a tree
Then he flew
I thought at me
Felt the gentle
Rapids flow
Oh, my
Is it really time to go
Such a beautiful day to end
But the fun
I'm glad we've been
My children, me and thee

Works from 2008 forward.

Disillusioned

Whipped cream on hot chocolate
melting slowly
creating round swirls
waiting to be blended with the chocolate below
does it then any longer have a separate identity
Left over snow in small drifts with mud at
its edges waiting for the sun to finish the work of melting
Loads of clothes waiting to be washed in hopes of
bleaching out this sulky disposition and the stains
that threaten to set in for life

Indecision

**I think of the warm bed and you next to me like a small
steady heater throughout the night
Can I give that up?
Is it that I am making a mountain from a mole hill over this?
A large investment of time and energy you have put into
the families now in the valley or
your lack of attention to or concern for me and your
consideration of us
that until a few months ago seemed to have existed in our
home
or does this pain speak to the larger problems that have existed
for awhile that I haven't wanted to see and cannot seem to face
You see no problems but at least are aware you are
experiencing cravings
Now when you are drinking often I feel like the you I know is
no longer there
I don't feel like I want to be near you and that sense of
this dark shadow that use to cover my soul is hovering just
around the corner
I can't stand the shadow and I don't wish to ever be that
close to the darkness again.
There is so much to lose and little to gain by the path you seem
to have chosen and it is one I cannot stand to travel with you
I hope this load soon lightens**

Roller Coaster Ride

I left but took much of the pain and confusion with me
I would do fine for two or three days then I would bounce back and forth like a volleyball within the confines of my brain
Where should I be, what should I do
Is it that I missed you or was it the safety that a marriage can provide
or maybe both
When we were together and things were stable I did not often have to look at myself in the mirror
or feel pushed nor encouraged by you to make changes for me or for us
I compromised often thinking that's what I should do in a marriage
and maybe it is
but not to the limits that I gave out of desperation
I more and more began to lose myself and to compromise what I felt had value in this life
to turn my head when there were wrongs I saw where I could not force a change
or make corrections for them
It seemed to do no good to point them out so it was either accept it, live with it or be forced to recognize I needed to step out of it
I can look back now and see to move out was right
but when I first left all I knew was I felt pain and I wanted it to stop
Hence I did come back for 36 hours and told you of the things that
would have to be different in order for me to at least consider coming back to stay
I gave all I had to give and left it on the doorstep
You gave words and no changes

then threats to make an end to yourself
I called the preacher and asked for him to counsel you
He insisted we both be there
It was not pretty and to me it became clear we were on opposite sides of a chasm
I called you for lunch and we talked
I stated our black and white differences
You still saw no need for changes and were set in how you viewed the events of the last year
I saw from my perspective
and it seemed the two versions would never find a midpoint at which to form a juncture
I and you needed to move forward with life
I sought a statement from you there would be no more threats to die
which you gave
Now perhaps the roller coaster would slow down
At least I do not feel the nose of your potential demise around my neck

Rises and falls before spiritual healing can begin

Cloudy days and restless nights
often drenched in sweat and froth with confusion
Bouncing
from one wall to the other within the confines of my mind
Choices made then second guessed
Will I, Want I, How can I, How can I not
Will there ever be enough
Faith in what I choose
Satisfaction in what I do

Acceptance of limits set
as being simply what they are and not in response to imagined flaws within myself
Carded wool
Chunks of wood and brambles
teased out along with soot and leafs
what is left is prettier and more useful
lighter
cleaner
purer
Purity
Can I remember a time and what it felt like?
Only as a young child.
How do I understand and pull lessons at my age
that should have come in adolescence
Healing Yes
How far I have come but
Dare I look too hard at what might be left to do
Then I might turn around and run rather then travel
the rocky road ahead
What halts my retreat
A single flame and beam of hope that I can learn this lesson
of independence and friendship before the opportunity retreats from my view
So many times I have driven away what I had come to consider so precious
because I did not understand how to share a common ground
Is it that I focus so much on the physical because I am so
afraid of the feelings and what feelings can mean
How much does it have to do with the fear of being abandoned
or my
Fear of abandoning someone else
Such guilt still

Have I for years hidden in a marriage of convenience so I was safe
from the need to know or the desire to address the truth
Knowledge ever powerful and frightening
Even now I can be so alone in a crowd
depending on the focus of my mind
I would hide again but
after writing the book and facing you I cannot
You mirrored what I could do and that I could be more if I choose to be
(I can hope I have done some of the same for you).
For once I must face this fear head on and hope this time to get beyond
the boundaries of my own soul
Regardless of where it leads I cannot go back
Defenses are coming down
So you see my friend I am between the proverbial rock and hard place
and find I must grow again
even though it is not easy to do

Roads to the past connecting to the present
Trains of thought
to the past
to the abuse
that apparently
became my connection
to knowing I was real
Then the sacrifice of another's innocence
to recreate that stage
even as a child could I have not made another choice
that would have prevented

the ripples of pain
that go on to this day
Now I am asked
to embrace that part of myself
that made that first choice
so many years ago
in order to move on
Is that not in some way saying
the choices
the acts that occurred
were acceptable
The question is can I live with this?
So now I must turn loose of all distractions
which means to forgo a lifetime of habits
death would almost be easier in spite of pain it
might cause others
Is it really worth all of this inner work
Can I deal with all this baggage of anger
that I constantly throw at myself
I am asking myself that question
and know there is a part of me that
wants to survive and pull together these
loose pieces to be one whole
oh the doubts
they are numerous and heavy
and she says to me
what do you do for self to replenish your own soul
and I am at a wall to think of much
too used to thinking about others it is hard to think about
what I can and need to give myself
my own undivided attention it would seem is the first
on the priority list
less pity is probably high as well

acceptance lord where does that go and of what
that I can't have everything I think I want
that I don't need to grasp at tomorrow when today is at hand
that looking back does not always mean I have to grieve but
that grieving may be the only way to embrace and accept
losses and maybes that haven't come to be
that I am what I am
Wishing will not change the past and only work and
circumstance
may change our future

Boundaries

If you find I am too close to the edge of your borders please tell me so. For these are healthy steps I need to take in directions where I have never gone.

Many times I have focused from a tunnel point of view and am just now learning to broaden where I look and for what I seek in life.

I have come to understand that in the diversity of the self balance can be attained.

I have not always traversed this life in a healthy manner and would like to move forward with more faith that I can relate to others as a whole person rather than in fragments as I have in the past.

The solace of my soul out weight's the balance of the mistakes that I have made and I know that my life has been of value to me and to others.

Steps

Always steps
leading to or from who knows where or when
Steps
One in front of the other
At least moving somewhere
Even if through confusion
This is better than standing still
Steps
Up steep cliffs
To reach places
To at least stand in patches of the morning sun
Steps
Down to lower corridors'
And hidden rooms and caves
In out of the way places
To seek a measure of truth
Steps
Across the sometimes barren distance
Of a heart that's been shattered
And left to wilt but not quite die
Steps
To a place to reclaim a life
That's been tortured
And left with a gaping wound
That just seems to refuse to want to heal
Steps

Sometimes one forward
And two back
Knowing the ones backwards hold no real joy
Only fear and turmoil

Steps

Out of painful memories
To each new day that might be
Blessed with rays of hope
And summer breezes
Steps

Toward today
Instead of tomorrow
Next week
Next year

Steps
Sometimes feeling chained
To what has been
But also knowing the key to hope
Is to continue to make

The effort
To take those steps
Even if the full faith is still lacking
Of where those steps may lead

Acceptance

I looked upon the face of death today
Slow, steady and defined
Confusion flowed from the eyes of the one
On whom these destined wings have gently settled
And she says
Can it be that at 50 I have reached such a place
That I can no longer be the person I once was
How can I accept that which I cannot seem to change
And live with what there is that is left to me
Some tell me to take what quality there is and
Not look so much at the quantity for that might drive me mad
I don't want pity handed in the guise of a caring friend
I want hope that perhaps there is a mistake in the coarse of the journey
that lies
Ahead of me
If not hope at least understanding and support for the truths
That I must face

Precipice

The nets are thrown far and wide this night
And I wonder if I can seek a new route and keep my wits about me
I don't want to veer too close to the outer edge of sadness
I have just barely gotten back on the level seas again
but I feel the need to start back on this journey forward
I am another year older come morning sun
And would hope at least a little wiser though I sometimes question if I can still partake of the experience of being wise
Often I have dreams of the past and our home on the boulevard
With tenuous strands that lead to now
I am wary of closeness and burned from what I have often felt
I am such a fool sometimes for such intense wanting and hoping
that I can find happiness I can share with another
I waste my own time in daydreams
Of an idealistic and probably unrealistic vision
The sands of time are moving on
perhaps I just need to stop having hope for things that may never come to be
Especially where you are concerned

Faith

It's raining and I hear the patter of heavy drops splashing on the window seal.

I listen to Elton John as he sings out the blues on a Tuesday night and at this moment I am satisfied with the place and time I have reached in this life.

I find no scabs or raw spots in my mind or on my body from the recent turmoil with which I have dealt.

Sometimes a few continued shadows drift across the sky, my face and soul.

I know they will for a time but I also know they will and do move on if I will let them do so.

I cannot change the world nor the fate of those I would choose to help, as the direction of each person's life is in his or her own hands.

I have accepted that knowledge though it has been a difficult task.

Tomorrow is fresh parchment on which to write beautiful words of hope if I am open to making that choice.

I have no idea how many pages are left for me to fill but I don't want to waste that gift of time looking so much back to the past or making negative conjectures toward the future.

I will breathe a full and deep breath for this moment and will gaze with open eyes at whatever the next moment brings.

I will use these thoughts as reminders of my hope when the shadows cross my life and for a time darken the sky.

Gratitude

The main theme of the book is how I personally dealt with, and have generally tried to move beyond, living with shame, and as only a survivor of mental, physical and sexual abuse.

To do this manuscript justice and offer as much support as possible to myself and others, I have tried to face areas of my life that remained generally hidden and unresolved. I knew the issues were there, and at times had felt overwhelmed by guilt for past behaviors that had the potential for long term negative effects on others. With this consideration in mind, I would therefore like to make the following acknowledgments.

I express my gratitude to a mother who made the choice to keep me even though my biological father tried to force her to abort her pregnancy. She had lost her own mother when she was 15, and said she could not bear to purposefully destroy this child she had conceived. I know due to many of your own life experiences, there have been times you have walked the brittle edge of sanity. It was difficult for me, as a child, to understand and accept your instability. After many years of life, I now have a better appreciation of the emotional and mental upheaval you had to face in your own childhood and later in your adult life. I thank you for keeping me alive, and hope for you it was worth the efforts.

I give my continued apologies to a brother who, due in part to my actions, also lost a childhood. I am sorry for many aspects of your life that might have been different if I had not, as a child, followed the example I experienced, and abused you secondary to my own molestation. I know all of us as children lived through having been born to parents who themselves had an unstable past, and exhibited intense mental health issues of their own. I know too that there are different expectations for men then there are for women, and it is even more difficult for males to acknowledge problems caused by childhood abuse. As an adult, I hoped you would be open to suggested treatment, but you have generally refused that route to recovery. When the subject has been approached, your response has always been to say there are no continuing effects from being abused, or growing up in a dysfunctional family. You know I disagree, but I realize I can only encourage healing choices, and I cannot make your choices for you. I know you will deal with your life in your own way and that there are many different paths to recovery. I hope for you and yours the best possible outcome in life that can be achieved.

To my son William, from whom I've been estranged for many years, I owe some explanations I may never be able to fully provide. I cannot explain away why I was not there for you the different times you felt I let you down. I am sorry for the many mistakes I made as a parent, and for some of the resulting anger you carry toward me and the world. I am in hopes that some day, and for your own sake, you will grow beyond the anger and take whatever steps are required to heal your own life. You work at a regular job and put money into the home where you live. That is a lot more accomplishment then many people can claim. I wish for you the best life has to offer. I wish you happiness, and hope someday for a reconciliation for the both of us. Time alone will tell but I think we have at least made those initial steps that it takes toward that recovery.

To my son John, who by his actions also demanded his independence at the early age of 16, I realize I am also accountable. We have processed a number of issues, and though I doubt that we will ever resolve them all, at least we have tried. Turning loose of your brother and you at such young ages, and within a year of each other, was not easy, but I did not seem to have a lot of choice in the matter. Not attempting to rescue either of you from consequences of your actions has been one of the hardest task of my life. It was probably one of the wisest choices I ever made. I am only now coming to understand that you had many more negative childhood experiences yourself than I had realized. I am still seeking to understand the depth of those experiences, but recognize that they have effected how you perceive, and currently live your own life. My hopes for you are that you survive your journey to recovery, and experience a level of learning and internal Peace as you go. I love you still but it may take time for us to be able to really connect again.

To my former husband Kenneth, I give my gratitude for our many years of struggle, learning and achievements. You always encouraged me to do whatever in life I wanted to do, and during our early time together, you did not hesitate to support me in any challenge I approached. Even with our Mars and Venus differences, you were often my harbor of safety when there was a need. It took time to settle into marital traces and learn to pull together. For both of us, I think it was worth the struggle and wait to reach that point in life. I am glad we shared a time of success. I was very saddened when our paths separated and we veered into opposite directions. It took me two years of steady struggle to finally come to terms with that loss and face life from a healthier perspective. Had it not been for the support of many friends and a new perspective on personal faith, I am not sure I would have successfully surfaced from that struggle. For you see, I loved you dearly, and had difficulty letting go of my unrealistic perception of you and our life together. I truly missed the closeness and caring we, at one time, had achieved. I finally realized that once it was gone it could not be reshaped or reestablished. That is a lesson it seems to have taken me a lifetime to learn.